Congressional
Research
Service

SBA Small Business Investment Company Program

Robert Jay Dilger
Senior Specialist in American National Government

December 11, 2012

Congressional Research Service

7-5700

www.crs.gov

R41456

CRS Report for Congress
Prepared for Members and Committees of Congress

Summary

The Small Business Administration's (SBA's) Small Business Investment Company (SBIC) Program is designed to enhance small business access to venture capital by stimulating and supplementing "the flow of private equity capital and long term loan funds which small business concerns need for the sound financing of their business operations and for their growth, expansion, and modernization, and which are not available in adequate supply." Facilitating the flow of capital to small businesses to stimulate the national economy was, and remains, the SBIC program's primary objective.

At the end of FY2012, there were 301 privately owned and managed SBICs licensed by the SBA, providing financing to small businesses with private capital the SBIC has raised (called regulatory capital) and funds the SBIC borrows at favorable rates (called leverage) because the SBA guarantees the debenture (loan obligation). SBICs pursue investments in a broad range of industries, geographic areas, and stages of investment. Some SBICs specialize in a particular field or industry, while others invest more generally. Most SBICs concentrate on a particular stage of investment (i.e., startup, expansion, or turnaround) and geographic area.

The SBA is authorized to provide up to $3 billion in leverage to SBICs annually. The SBIC program has invested or committed about $18.2 billion in small businesses, with the SBA's share of capital at risk about $8.8 billion. In FY2012, the SBA committed to guarantee $1.9 billion in SBIC small business investments, and SBICs provided another $1.3 billion in investments from private capital, for a total of more than $3.2 billion in financing for 1,094 small businesses.

Some Members of Congress, the Obama Administration, and small business advocates argue that the program should be expanded as a means to stimulate economic activity, create jobs, and assist in the national economic recovery. For example, S. 3442, the SUCCESS Act of 2012, and S. 3572, the Restoring Tax and Regulatory Certainty to Small Businesses Act of 2012, would, among other provisions, increase the program's authorization amount to $4 billion from $3 billion, increase the program's family of funds limit (the amount of outstanding leverage allowed for two or more SBIC licenses under common control) to $350 million from $225 million, and annually adjust the maximum outstanding leverage amount available to both individual SBICs and SBICs under common control to account for inflation. Also, H.R. 6504, the Small Business Investment Company Modernization Act of 2012, would increase the program's family of funds limit (the amount of outstanding leverage allowed for two or more SBIC licenses under common control) to $350 million from $225 million.

Others worry that an expanded SBIC program could result in loses and increase the federal deficit. In their view, the best means to assist small business, promote economic growth, and create jobs is to reduce business taxes and exercise federal fiscal restraint.

Some Members have also proposed that the program target additional assistance to startup and early stage small businesses, which are generally viewed as relatively risky investments but also as having a relatively high potential for job creation. In an effort to target additional assistance to newer businesses, the SBA has established, as part of the Obama Administration's Startup America Initiative, a $1 billion early stage debenture SBIC initiative (up to $150 million in leverage in FY2012, and up to $200 million in leverage per fiscal year thereafter until the limit is reached). Early stage debenture SBICs are required to invest at least 50% of their investments in early stage small businesses, defined as small businesses that have never achieved positive cash flow from operations in any fiscal year.

This report describes the SBIC program's structure and operations, including two recent SBA initiatives, one targeting early stage small businesses and one targeting underserved markets. It also examines several legislative proposals to increase the leverage available to SBICs and to increase the SBIC program's authorization amount to $4 billion.

Contents

Tables

Appendixes

Contacts

SBIC Program Overview

The Small Business Administration (SBA) administers several programs to support small businesses, including loan guaranty programs to enhance small business access to capital; programs to increase small business opportunities in federal contracting; direct loans for businesses, homeowners, and renters to assist their recovery from natural disasters; and access to entrepreneurial education to assist with business formation and expansion.[1] It also administers the Small Business Investment Company (SBIC) Program.

Authorized by P.L. 85-699, the Small Business Investment Act of 1958, as amended, the SBIC program is designed to "improve and stimulate the national economy in general and the small business segment thereof in particular" by stimulating and supplementing "the flow of private equity capital and long term loan funds which small business concerns need for the sound financing of their business operations and for their growth, expansion, and modernization, and which are not available in adequate supply."[2]

The SBIC program was created to address concerns raised in a Federal Reserve Board report to Congress that concluded that a gap existed in the capital markets for long-term funding for growth-oriented small businesses. The report noted that the SBA's loan programs were "limited to providing short-term and intermediate-term credit when such loans are unavailable from private institutions," and the SBA "did not provide equity financing."[3] Equity financing (or equity capital) is money raised by a company in exchange for a share of ownership in the business. Ownership is represented by owning shares of stock outright or having the right to convert other financial instruments into stock. Equity financing allows a business to obtain funds without incurring debt, or without having to repay a specific amount of money at a particular time. The Federal Reserve Board's report concluded that there was a need for a federal government program to "stimulate the availability of capital funds to small business" to assist them in gaining access to long-term financing and equity financing.[4] Facilitating the flow of capital to small businesses to stimulate the national economy was, and remains, the SBIC program's primary objective.

The SBA does not make direct investments in small businesses. It partners with privately owned and managed SBICs licensed by the SBA to provide financing to small businesses with private capital the SBIC has raised (called regulatory capital) and with funds (called leverage) the SBIC borrows at favorable rates because the SBA guarantees the debenture (loan obligation). At the end of FY2012, there were 301 licensed SBICs participating in the SBIC program.[5]

The SBA is authorized to provide up to $3 billion in leverage to SBICs annually. In FY2012, the SBA provided $1.9 billion in leverage to SBICs.[6]

---

[1] U.S. Small Business Administration, "Fiscal Year 2013 Congressional Budget Justification and FY2011 Annual Performance Report," p. 1.

[2] 15 U.S.C. §661.

[3] U.S. Congress, House Committee on Banking and Currency, *Small Business Investment Act of 1958*, report to accompany S.3651, 85th Cong., 2nd sess., June 30, 1958, H.Rept. 85-2060 (Washington: GPO, 1958), pp. 4, 5.

[4] Ibid., p. 5.

[5] U.S. Small Business Administration, "SBIC Program Overview, as of September 30, 2012," at http://c.ymcdn.com/ sites/www.sbia.org/resource/resmgr/Docs/SBIC_Program_Overview.pdf.

[6] Ibid.

Some Members of Congress, the Obama Administration, and small business advocates have argued that the SBIC program should be expanded as a means to stimulate economic activity, create jobs, and assist in the national economic recovery. For example, S. 3442, the SUCCESS Act of 2012, and S. 3572, the Restoring Tax and Regulatory Certainty to Small Businesses Act of 2012, would, among other provisions, increase the program's authorization amount to $4 billion from $3 billion, increase the program's family of funds limit (the amount of outstanding SBA leverage allowed for two or more SBIC licenses under common control) to $350 million from $225 million, and annually adjust the maximum outstanding SBA leverage amount available to both individual SBICs and SBIC investments under common control to account for inflation.[7] Also, H.R. 6504, the Small Business Investment Company Modernization Act of 2012, would increase the program's family of funds limit to $350 million from $225 million.[8]

Others worry about the potential risk an expanded SBIC program has for increasing the federal deficit. In their view, the best means to assist small business, promote economic growth, and create jobs is to reduce business taxes and exercise federal fiscal restraint.

Some Members and small business advocates have also proposed that the program target additional assistance to startup and early stage small businesses, which are generally viewed as relatively risky investments but also as having a relatively high potential for job creation. The SBA, in an effort to target additional assistance to newer businesses, recently established, as part of the Administration's Startup America Initiative, a $1 billion early stage debenture SBIC initiative (up to $150 million in leverage in FY2012, and up to $200 million in leverage per fiscal year thereafter until the limit is reached). Early stage debenture SBICs are required to invest at least 50% of their investments in early stage small businesses, defined as small businesses that have never achieved positive cash flow from operations in any fiscal year.

This report examines the structure and operation of the SBIC program, focusing on SBIC eligibility requirements, investment activity, and program statistics. It includes information concerning the SBIC program's debenture SBIC program, participating securities SBIC program, $1 billion early stage debenture SBIC initiative (targeting early stage small businesses), and $1 billion impact investment SBIC initiative (targeting underserved markets and communities facing barriers to access to credit and capital).

This report also examines proposals and legislation considered during the 111th and 112th Congresses, including H.R. 3854, the Small Business Financing and Investment Act of 2009; H.R. 5554, the Small Business Assistance and Relief Act of 2010; P.L. 111-240, the Small Business Jobs Act of 2010; H.R. 6504, the Small Business Investment Company Modernization Act of 2012; S.Amdt. 1833, the INVEST in America Act of 2012; S. 3442, the SUCCESS Act of 2012, S. 3572, the Restoring Tax and Regulatory Certainty to Small Businesses Act of 2012,

---

[7] S. 2136, a bill to increase the maximum amount of leverage permitted under title III of the Small Business Investment Act of 1958, and for other purposes, would increase the SBIC program's authorization amount to $4 billion from $3 billion, and increase the program's family of funds limit (the amount of outstanding leverage allowed for two or more SBIC licenses under common control) to $350 million from $225 million.

[8] H.R. 3219, the Small Business Investment Company Modernization Act of 2011, the processor bill to H.R. 6504, the Small Business Investment Company Modernization Act of 2012, also would increase the SBIC program's family of funds limit (the amount of outstanding leverage allowed for two or more SBIC licenses under common control) to $350 million from $225 million.

and the Obama Administration's Startup America Initiative. These proposals and legislation address the program's financing and/or the targeting of additional assistance to startup and early stage small businesses.

SBIC Types

There are two types of SBICs. Investment companies licensed under Section 301(c) of the Small Business Investment Act of 1958, as amended, are referred to as original, or regular, SBICs. Investment companies licensed under Section 301(d) of the act, called Specialized Small Business Investment Companies (SSBICs), focus on providing financing to small business entrepreneurs "whose participation in the free enterprise system is hampered because of social or economic disadvantage."[9] Section 301(d) was repealed by P.L. 104-208, the Omnibus Consolidated Appropriations Act, 1997 (Title II of Division D, the Small Business Programs Improvement Act of 1996). As a result, no new SSBIC licenses have been issued since October 1, 1996. However, existing SSBICs were "grandfathered" and remain in operation.

With few exceptions, SBICs and SSBICs are subject to the same eligibility requirements and operating rules and regulations. Therefore, the SBIC name is usually used to refer to both SBICs and SSBICs simultaneously.

There are five types of regular SBICs. *Debenture* SBICs, *impact investment debenture* SBICs, and *early stage debenture* SBICs receive leverage through the issuance of debentures.[10] Debentures are debt obligations issued by SBICs and held or guaranteed by the SBA.[11] *Participating securities* SBICs receive leverage through the issuance of participating securities. Participating securities are redeemable, preferred, equity-type securities, often in the form of limited partnership interests, preferred stock, or debentures with interest payable only to the extent of earnings.[12] *Bank-owned, non-leveraged* SBICs do not receive leverage.[13] This report focuses on the four types of regular SBICs that receive leverage from the SBA.

SBIC Eligibility Requirements

An SBIC can be organized in any state, as either a corporation, limited partnership (LP), or a limited liability company (LLCs must be organized under Delaware law). Most SBICs are owned by relatively small groups of local investors, although many are partially owned, and some are

---

[9] P.L. 92-595, the Small Business Investment Act Amendments of 1972.

[10] A debenture SBIC may issue and have outstanding both guaranteed debentures and participating securities, provided that the total amount of participating securities outstanding does not exceed 200% of its private capital. See 13 CFR §107.1170. The SBA stopped issuing new commitments for participating securities on October 1, 2004.

[11] 13 CFR §107.50.

[12] Ibid.

[13] Commercial banks may invest up to 5% of their capital and surplus to partially or wholly own an SBIC. Bank investments in an SBIC are presumed by federal regulatory agencies to be a "qualified investment" for Community Reinvestment Act purposes. See P.L. 90-104, the Small Business Act Amendments of 1967; The Board of Governors of the Federal Reserve Board, "Small Business Investment Companies," 33 *Federal Register* 6967, May 9, 1968; and U.S. Small Business Administration, "Small Business Investment Companies (SBICs)," *Small Business Notes*, 2009, at http://www.smallbusinessnotes.com/financing/sbic.html.

---

wholly owned (44 of 301), by commercial banks. A few SBICs are corporations with publicly traded stock.[14]

One of the primary criteria for licensure as an SBIC is having qualified management. The SBA reviews and approves a prospective SBIC's management team based upon its professional capabilities and character. Specifically, the SBA examines the SBIC's management team looking for

- substantive and relevant principal investment experience;

- realized track record of superior returns, based on an overall evaluation of appropriate quantitative performance measures;

- evidence of a strong rate of business proposals and investment offers (deal flow) in the investment area proposed for the new fund;

- a cohesive management team, with complementary skills and history of working together;

- managerial, operational, or technical experience that can add value at the portfolio company level; and

- a demonstrated ability to manage cash flows so as to provide assurance the SBA will be repaid on a timely basis.[15]

SBIC Application Process

Applying for an SBIC debenture license is a multi-step process, beginning with the submission of the SBA Management Assessment Questionnaire (MAQ). It includes, among others, questions concerning

- the fund's legal name, and the name and addresses of its principals and control persons;[16]

- the fund's finances and expenses;

- the management team's professional experience;

- the fund's expected investing focus (e.g., will the fund be primarily a sole investor, lead investor, or co-investor; its anticipated percentage of investments in technology, life sciences, health care, manufacturing, distribution, service, consumer products and retail, or other industries; and its anticipated percentage of investments by business life cycle—seed, early stage, expansion, later stage, change of control, or turnaround);

- the geographic areas where the investments are expected to be made;

---

[14] U.S. Small Business Administration, "For SBIC Applicants: Phase II: Licensing Review," at http://www.sba.gov/content/phase-ii-licensing-review.

[15] U.S. Small Business Administration, "For SBIC Applicants: Pre-Screening," at http://www.sba.gov/content/pre-screening.

[16] A control person is generally defined as someone with the power to direct corporate management and policies.

- the anticipated holding periods for investments;
- the types and characteristics of the securities that will be used to make investments; and
- the extent to which "special groups of businesses" will be targeted for investment, such as "ethnic groups, women, rural, inner city, etc."[17]

After receiving the firm's application, a member of the SBA's Program Development Office reviews the MAQ; assesses the investment company's proposal in light of the program's minimum requirements and management qualifications; performs initial due diligence, including making reference telephone calls; and prepares a written recommendation to the SBA's Investment Division's Investment Committee (composed of senior members of the division).

If, after reviewing the MAQ and the SBA's Program Development Office's evaluation, the Investment Committee concludes, by majority vote at a regularly scheduled meeting, that the investment company's management team may be qualified for a license, the investment company's management team is invited to the SBA's headquarters in Washington, DC, for an interview. If, following the interview, the Investment Committee votes to proceed, the investment team is provided a "Green Light" letter, formally inviting the investment team to file a license application, along with a filing fee of $10,000, plus an additional $5,000 for partnerships or LLC SBICs. If the license is approved, all SBIC principals must complete the SBA's SBIC Regulations training classes. On average, obtaining an SBIC license takes about six months from the time of the initial submission of the MAQ to issuance of the license.[18]

As will be discussed, new applications for the participating securities program are no longer being accepted. Impact investment debenture SBIC applicants are required to submit the same documents, follow the same process, and meet the same standards as applicants seeking a debenture SBIC license. However, impact investment debenture SBICs are provided an expedited review process.[19]

The application process for an early stage debenture SBIC license is similar to the application process for a SBIC debenture license. Two major differences are that the SBA only accepts applications to the early stage innovation program during specific time periods published "from time to time" in the *Federal Register* (expected to be annually) and places "particular emphasis on managers' skills and experience in evaluating and investing in early stage companies."[20] Also, early stage debenture SBIC applicants must pay a partnership licensee fee plus an additional $10,000, for a total application fee of $25,000.[21]

---

[17] U.S. Small Business Administration, "SBIC Management Assessment Questionnaire and License Application: Form 2181," p. 21, at http://www.sba.gov/sites/default/files/SBA%20Form%202181.pdf.

[18] U.S. Small Business Administration, "SBIC Program Statistics & Administrative Performance," at http://www.sba.gov/content/program-statistics-administrative-performance#LicTimes; and U.S. Small Business Administration, Office of Congressional and Legislative Affairs, "Correspondence with the author," September 21, 2010.

[19] U.S. Small Business Administration, "Impact Investment Initiative," at http://www.sba.gov/content/small-business-investment-company-sbic-impact-investment-initiative-2.

[20] U.S. Small Business Administration, "Small Business Investment Companies - Early Stage SBICs," 77 *Federal Register* 25052, April 27, 2012.

[21] Ibid.

The eligibility requirements and application process for small businesses requesting financial assistance from an SBIC is provided in the **Appendix**.

SBIC Capital Investment Requirements

Debenture SBICs

P.L. 85-699, the Small Business Investment Act of 1958, authorized the SBA to select companies to participate in the SBIC program and to purchase debentures from those companies to provide them additional funds to invest in small businesses. Initially, debenture SBICs were required to have a private capital investment of at least $300,000 to participate in the SBIC program.

Debenture SBICs are now required to have a private capital investment of at least $5 million (called regulatory capital).[22] The SBA has discretion to license an applicant with regulatory capital of $3 million if the applicant has satisfied all licensing standards and requirements, has a viable business plan reasonably projecting profitable operations, and has a reasonable timetable for achieving regulatory capital of at least $5 million.[23] At least 30% of a debenture SBIC's regulatory and leverageable capital must come from three people unaffiliated with the fund's management and unaffiliated with each other.[24] Also, no more than 33% of a SBIC's regulatory capital may come from state or local government entities.[25]

Participating Securities SBICs

P.L. 102-366, the Small Business Credit and Business Opportunity Enhancement Act of 1992 (Title IV, the Small Business Equity Enhancement Act of 1992), authorized the SBA to guarantee participating securities. Participating securities are redeemable, preferred, equity-type securities issued by SBICs in the form of limited partnership interests, preferred stock, or debentures with interest payable only to the extent of earnings.

In 1994, the SBA established the SBIC Participating Securities Program (SBIC PSP) to encourage the formation of participating securities SBICs that would make equity investments in startup and early stage small businesses. The SBA created the program to fill a perceived investment gap created by the SBIC debenture program's focus on mid- and later-stage small businesses. The SBA stopped issuing new commitments for participation securities on October 1, 2004, beginning a process to end the program, which continues.[26]

The SBA stopped issuing new commitments for participating securities primarily because the program experienced a projected loss of $2.7 billion during the early 2000s as investments in

---

[22] 13 CFR §107.210.

[23] Ibid.

[24] 13 CFR §107.150.

[25] 13 CFR §107.230.

[26] U.S. Congress, House Committee on Small Business, *Private Equity for Small Firms: The Importance of the Participating Securities Program*, 109th Cong., 1st sess., April 13, 2005, Serial No. 109-10 (Washington: GPO, 2005), p. 5, 33; and U.S. Small Business Administration, "SBIC Program: FAQs 7. What is the status of the Participating Securities Program?" at http://www.sba.gov/content/faqs.

technology startup and early stage small businesses lost much of their stock value at that time. The SBA found that "the fees payable by SBICs for participating securities leverage are not sufficient to cover the projected net losses in the participating securities program."[27] The SBA continued to honor its existing commitments to participating securities SBICs and they were allowed to continue operations. However, they were required to comply with special rules concerning minimum capital, liquidity, non-SBA borrowing, and equity investing.[28] In recent years, some Members have expressed interest in either revising the program or starting a new program modeled on certain aspects of the SBIC PSP to assist startup and early stage small businesses has increased.[29]

Although the SBA is no longer issuing new commitments for participating securities, and each year several participating securities SBICs leave the program as their leverage commitments are retired, at the end of FY2012 there were still 86 participating securities SBICs in the SBIC program.[30] To participate in the SBIC program, a participating securities SBICs must have regulatory capital of at least $10 million. The SBA has discretion to require less than $10 million in regulatory capital if the licensee can demonstrate that it can be financially viable over the long term with a lower amount. In this circumstance, the regulatory amount required may not be lower than $5 million.[31] At least 30% of a participating securities SBIC's regulatory and leverageable capital must come from three people unaffiliated with the fund's management and unaffiliated with each other.[32] Also, no more than 33% of a SBIC's regulatory capital can come from state or local government entities.[33]

---

[27] U.S. Small Business Administration, "Offering Circular, Guaranteed 4.727% Participating Securities Participation Certificates, Series SBIC-PS 2009-10 A," February 19, 2009, at http://www.sba.gov/content/sbic-ps-2009-10-cusip-831641-ep6.

[28] 13 CFR §107.1500. A SBIC that wishes to be eligible to issue participating securities must have regulatory capital of at least $10 million unless it can demonstrate to the SBA's satisfaction that it can be financially viable over the long-term with a lower amount, but not less than $5 million. See 13 CFR §107.210. It must also maintain sufficient liquidity to avoid a condition of "Liquidity Impairment," defined as a liquidity ratio (total current funds available divided by total current funds required) of less than 1.2. See 13 CFR §107.1505. The only type of debt, other than leverage, than a SBIC that has applied to issue participating securities or have outstanding participating securities is permitted to incur is temporary debt. Temporary debt is defined as short-term borrowings from a regulated financial institution, a regulated credit company, or a non-regulated lender approved by the SBA for the purpose of maintaining the SBIC's operating liquidity or providing funds for a particular financing of a small business. The total outstanding borrowings, not including leverage, may not exceed 50% of a SBIC's leveraged capital and all such borrowings must be fully paid off for at least 30 consecutive days during a SBIC's fiscal year so that it has no outstanding third-party debt for 30 days. See 13 CFR §107.570. A SBIC issuing participating securities is required to invest an amount equal to the original issue price of such securities solely in equity capital investments (e.g., common or preferred stock, limited partnership interests, options, warrants, or similar equity instruments). See 13 CFR §107.1505.

[29] U.S. Congress, House Committee on Small Business, *Subcommittee Markup of Legislation Affecting the SBA Capital Access Programs*, 111th Cong., 1st sess., October 8, 2009, House Small Business Committee Document No. 111-050 (Washington: GPO, 2009), pp. 7, 10, 11, 187-194; U.S. Congress, House Committee on Small Business, *Full Committee Hearing on Increasing Capital for Small Business*, 111th Cong., 1st sess., October 14, 2009, House Small Business Committee Document No. 111-051 (Washington: GPO, 2009), pp. 1, 2, 40, 98; and U.S. Congress, House Committee on Small Business, *Small Business Financing and Investment Act of 2009*, report to accompany H.R. 3854, 111th Cong., 1st sess., October 26, 2009, H.Rept. 111-315 (Washington: GPO, 2009), pp. 3, 4, 10-12.

[30] U.S. Small Business Administration, "SBIC Program Overview, as of September 30, 2012," at http://c.ymcdn.com/ sites/www.sbia.org/resource/resmgr/Docs/SBIC_Program_Overview.pdf. There were 149 participating securities SBICs at the end of FY2008.

[31] 13 CFR §107.210.

[32] 13 CFR §107.150.

[33] 13 CFR §107.230.

Impact Investment Debenture SBICs

On April 7, 2011, the SBA announced that it was establishing a $1 billion impact investment SBIC initiative (up to $150 million in leverage in FY2012, and up to $200 million in leverage per fiscal year thereafter until the limit is reached). Under this initiative, SBA-licensed impact investment debenture SBICs are required to invest at least 50% of their financings, "which target areas of critical national priority including underserved markets and communities facing barriers to access to credit and capital."[34] Impact investment debenture SBICs are required to have a minimum private capital investment of at least $5 million, subject to the same conditions as debenture SBICs concerning the source of the funds.

At the end of FY2012, two impact investment SBICs had been licensed and four standard debenture SBICs had an impact focus. The SBA reported that these funds have over $200 million in private capital and close to $400 million of SBA-guaranteed leverage to make impact investments.[35]

Early Stage Debenture SBICs

On April 27, 2012, the SBA published a final rule in the *Federal Register* establishing a $1 billion early stage debenture SBIC initiative (up to $150 million in leverage in FY2012, and up to $200 million in leverage per fiscal year thereafter until the limit is reached).[36] Early stage debenture SBICs are required to invest at least 50% of their financings in early stage small businesses, defined as small businesses that have never achieved positive cash flow from operations in any fiscal year.[37]

In recognition of the higher risk associated with investments in early stage small businesses, the initiative includes "several new regulatory provisions intended to reduce the risk that an early stage SBIC would default on its leverage and to improve SBA's recovery prospects should a default occur."[38] For example, early stage debenture SBICs are required to raise more regulatory capital (at least $20 million) than debenture SBICs and impact investment debenture SBICs (at least $5 million) and participating securities SBICs (at least $10 million). They are also subject to special distribution rules to require pro rata repayment of SBA leverage when making

---

[34] U.S. Small Business Administration, "Impact Investment Initiative," at http://www.sba.gov/content/small-business-investment-company-sbic-impact-investment-initiative-2. To receive an investment, a small business must meet at least one of the following criteria: (a) it must be located in, or have at least 35% of its full-time employees, at the time of the initial investment, residing in a low or moderate income area as defined in 13 CFR §107.50; or be located in an economically distressed area as defined by Section 3011 of the Public Works and Economic Development Act of 1965, as amended [per capita income of 80% or less of the national average or an unemployment rate that is, for the most recent 24-month period for which data are available, at least 1% greater than the national average unemployment rate]; or (b) be in an industrial sector that the SBA has identified as a national priority (currently clean energy and education). The SBA has announced that additional industrial sectors will be added over time in partnership with other mission-driven agencies.

[35] U.S. Small Business Administration, "The Small Business Investment Company (SBIC) Program: Annual Report FY2012," p. 19, at http://www.sba.gov/sites/default/files/files/SBIC%20Program%20FY%202012%20Annual%20Report.pdf.

[36] U.S. Small Business Administration, "Small Business Investment Companies - Early Stage SBICs," 77 *Federal Register* 25043, 25050, April 27, 2012.

[37] Ibid., pp. 25051-25053.

[38] Ibid., p. 25043.

---

distributions of profits to their investors. In addition, as will be discussed, early stage debenture SBICs are also provided less leverage (up to 100% of regulatory capital, $50 million maximum) than debenture SBICs and participating securities SBICs (up to 200% of regulatory capital, $150 million maximum per SBIC and $225 million for two or more SBICs under common control), and impact investment debenture SBICs (up to 200% of regulatory capital, $80 million maximum).

On May 1, 2012, the SBA published a notice in the *Federal Register* inviting venture capital fund managers to submit an application to become a licensed early stage debenture SBIC. The application deadline for applicants with signed commitments for at least $15 million in regulatory capital and evidence of their ability to raise the remaining $5 million in regulatory capital was set as July 30, 2012. The application deadline for all other applicants was set as May 15, 2013.[39] Thirty-three venture capital funds submitted preliminary application materials to participate in the program. After these materials were examined and interviews held, the SBA announced on October 23, 2012, that it had issued "green light" letters to six funds, formally inviting these funds to file a license application.[40]

Key Differences Among Regular SBIC Types

Table 1 provides a comparison of the key differences among the four types of regular SBICs that receive leverage from the SBA: debenture, participating securities, impact investment debenture, and early stage debenture SBICs.

Table 1. Key Differences Among SBA's Debenture, Participating Securities, Impact Investment Debenture, and Early Stage Debenture SBICs

Program Requirement	Debenture SBICs	Participating Security SBICs (no longer accepting new investments)	Impact Investment Debenture SBICs	Early Stage Debenture SBICs
Private Capital	$5 million minimum	$10 million minimum	$5 million minimum	$20 million minimum
SBA Leverage	200% of private capital up to $150 million per SBIC or $225 million for two or more SBICs under common control[a]	200% of private capital up to $150 million per SBIC or $225 million for two or more SBICs under common control	200% of private capital up to $80 million; limited to 100% of private capital during the first year	100% of private capital up to $50 million

---

[39] U.S. Small Business Administration, "Small Business Investment Companies - Early Stage SBICs," 77 *Federal Register* 25775-25779, May 1, 2012.

[40] U.S. Small Business Administration, "SBA's Growth Capital Program Sets Record For Third Year in a Row $2.95 Billion in Financing for Small Businesses in FY12," at http://www.sba.gov/about-sba-services/7367/342171; and U.S. Small Business Administration, "The Small Business Investment Company (SBIC) Program: Annual Report FY2012," p. 20, at http://www.sba.gov/sites/default/files/files/SBIC%20Program%20FY%202012%20Annual%20Report.pdf.

Program Requirement	Debenture SBICs	Participating Security SBICs (no longer accepting new investments)	Impact Investment Debenture SBICs	Early Stage Debenture SBICs
Investments	Broad range of equity investments, but generally later stage and mezzanine	Broad range of equity investments	Broad range of equity investments, but generally later stage and mezzanine; at least 50% in underserved markets and communities facing barriers to access to credit and capital	Broad range of equity investments; at least 50% in early stage small businesses (no positive cash flow in any fiscal year prior to first financing)
Leverage Description	Interest and SBA annual charge payable semi-annually through maturity	SBA paid interest to bond holders; SBICs only owed and repaid SBA out of profits	Interest and SBA annual charge payable semi-annually through maturity	Standard: 5 years interest reserve required, interest and SBA annual charge payable quarterly through maturity OR

Discounted: interest and SBA annual charge discounted for first 5 years plus the "stub" period; interest and SBA annual charge payable quarterly thereafter through maturity |
| Profit Participation | None | SBA typically received about 8% of any profits | None | None |

Source: U.S. Small Business Administration, Office of Investment and Innovation, "Early Stage Small Business Investment Companies," January 2012; and U.S. Small Business Administration, "Correspondence with the author," May 2, 2012.

a. A licensed debenture SBIC in good standing, with a demonstrated need for funds, may apply to the SBA for leverage of up to 300% of its private capital. However, the SBA has traditionally approved debenture SBICs for a maximum of 200% of their private capital. It is anticipated that the SBA will also limit impact investment debenture SBICs to a maximum of 200% of their private capital. Also, a debenture SBIC licensed on or after October 1, 2009, may elect to have a maximum leverage amount of $175 million per SBIC and $250 million for two or more licenses under common control if it has invested at least 50% of its financings in low-income geographic areas and certifies that at least 50% of its future investments will be in low-income geographic areas.

SBIC Investments in Small Businesses

SBICs provide equity capital to small businesses in various ways, including by

- purchasing small business equity securities (e.g., stock, stock options, warrants, limited partnership interests, membership interests in a limited liability company, or joint venture interests);[41]

- making loans to small businesses, either independently or in cooperation with other private or public lenders, that have a maturity of no more than 20 years;[42]

- purchasing debt securities from small businesses, which may be convertible into, or have rights to purchase, equity in the small business;[43] and

- subject to limitations, providing small businesses a guarantee of their monetary obligations to creditors not associated with the SBIC.[44]

SBICs are subject to statutory and regulatory restrictions concerning the nature of their approved investments. For example, SBICs are not allowed to

- directly or indirectly provide financing to any of their associates (e.g., officers, directors, and employees);[45]

- control, either directly or indirectly, any small business on a permanent basis;[46]

- invest, without SBA approval, more than specified percentages of its private (regulatory) capital in securities, commitments, or guarantees in any one small business (e.g., SBICs are not allowed to invest more than 30% of their private capital in any one small business if their investment plan includes two or more tiers of SBA leverage);[47]

- invest in farm land, unimproved land, or any small business classified under Major Group 65 (Real Estate) of the Standard Industrial Classification (SIC) Manual, with the exception of title abstract companies, real estate agents, brokers, and managers;[48]

---

[41] 13 CFR §107.800. A SBIC is not allowed to become a general partner in any unincorporated business or become jointly or severally liable for any obligations of an unincorporated business.

[42] 13 CFR §107.810; and 13 CFR §107.840.

[43] 13 CFR §107.815. Debt securities are instruments evidencing a loan with an option or any other right to acquire equity securities in a small business or its affiliates, or a loan which by its terms is convertible into an equity position, or a loan with a right to receive royalties that are excluded from the cost of money.

[44] 13 CFR §107.820.

[45] 13 CFR §107.730.

[46] 13 CFR §107.865. The period of time that a SBIC may exercise control over a small business for purposes connected with its investment through ownership of voting securities, management agreements, voting trusts, majority representation on the board of directors, or otherwise, is "limited to the seventh anniversary of the date on which such control was initially acquired, or any earlier date specified by the terms of any investment agreement." With the SBA's prior written approval, an SBIC "may retain control for such additional period as may be reasonably necessary to complete divestiture of control or to ensure the financial stability of the portfolio company."

[47] A tier of SBA leverage equals the amount of a SBIC's private (regulatory) capital. A SBIC approved for less than two tiers of SBA leverage must not invest more than 20% of its private capital in any one small business if the SBIC's plan contemplates one tier of leverage and no more than 25% of its private capital if its plan contemplates 1.5 tiers of leverage. See 13 CFR §107.740; and U.S. Small Business Administration, "American Recovery and Reinvestment Act of 2009: Implementation of SBIC Program Changes," letter from Harry Haskins, Acting Associate Administrator for Investment, to All Small Business Investment Companies (SBICs) and Applicants, May 4, 2009, p. 2, at http://archive.sba.gov/idc/groups/public/documents/sba_program_office/inv_rcvry_act_sbic_changes.pdf.

[48] 13 CFR §107.720.

- provide funds for small businesses whose primary business activity involves directly or indirectly providing funds to others, purchasing debt obligations, factoring, or leasing equipment on a long-term basis with no provision for maintenance or repair;[49] or

- provide funds to a small business if the funds will be used substantially for a foreign operation.[50]

The SBA also regulates the interest rates and fees SBICs are allowed to charge small businesses on loans, debt securities, and equity financing.[51]

In 1999, the SBA introduced the low and moderate income investments (LMI) initiative to encourage SBICs to invest in small businesses located in inner cities and rural areas "that have severe shortages of equity capital" because investments in those areas "often are of a type that will not have the potential for yielding returns that are high enough to justify the use of participating securities."[52] This ongoing initiative provides incentives to SBICs that invest in small businesses that have at least 50% of their employees or tangible assets located in a low-to-moderate income area (LMI Zone) or have at least 35% of their full-time employees with their primary residence in an LMI Zone.[53] For example, unlike regular SBIC debentures that typically have a 10-year maturity, LMI debentures are available in two maturities, for 5 years and 10 years, plus the stub period. The stub period is the time between the debenture's issuance date and the next March 1 or September 1. The stub period allows all LMI debentures to have common March 1 or September 1 maturity dates to simplify administration of the program.

In addition, LMI debentures are issued at a discount so that the proceeds that a SBIC receives for the sale of a debenture is reduced by (1) the debenture's interest costs for the first five years, plus the stub period; (2) the SBA's annual fee for the debenture's first five years, plus the stub period;

---

[49] Ibid.

[50] Ibid. A SBIC may provide venture capital financing to "disadvantaged concerns" engaged in relending or reinvesting activities (except agricultural credit companies and banking and savings and loan institutions not insured by a federal agency). Without SBA approval, these financings, at the end of the fiscal year, may not exceed a SBIC's regulatory capital. A disadvantaged concern is defined as a small business that is at least 50% owned, controlled, and managed, on a day-to-day basis, by a person or persons whose participation in the free enterprise system is hampered because of social or economic disadvantages.

[51] The SBA has a general interest rate ceiling of 19% for a loan and 14% for a debt security, with provisions for a higher interest rate under specified circumstances. See 13 CFR §107.855. A SBIC is allowed to collect a nonrefundable application fee of no more than 1% of the amount of financing requested from a small business to review its financing application, a closing fee of no more than 2% of the amount of financing requested from a small business concern for a loan, charged no earlier than the date of the first disbursement, and a closing fee of no more than 4% of the amount of financing requested from a small business concern for a debt security or equity security financing, charged no earlier than the date of the first disbursement. A SBIC is also allowed to charge a small business for reasonable out-of-pocket expenses, other than management expenses incurred to process the small business's financing application. See 13 CFR §107.860.

[52] U.S. Small Business Administration, "Small Business Investment Companies," 64 *Federal Register* 52645, September 30, 1999.

[53] U.S. Small Business Administration, "Small Business Investment Companies," 64 *Federal Register* 52641-52646, September 30, 1999. LMI Zones are areas located in a HUBZone; an Urban Empowerment Zone or Urban Enterprise Community designated by the Secretary of the U.S. Department of Housing and Urban Development; a Rural Empowerment Zone or Rural Enterprise Community as designated by the Secretary of the U.S. Department of Agriculture; an area of low income or moderate income as recognized by the Federal Financial Institutions Examination Council; or a county with persistent poverty as classified by the U.S. Department of Agriculture's Economic Research Service. See 13 CFR §107.50.

---

and (3) the SBA's 2% leverage fee. As a result, these interest costs and fees are effectively deferred, freeing SBICs from the requirement to make interest payments on LMI debentures, or pay the SBA's annual fees on LMI debentures, for the first five years of a debenture, plus the stub period between the debenture's issuance date and the next March 1 or September 1.[54]

In FY2012, SBICs made 356 investments in small businesses located in a LMI Zone, totaling $471.5 million—about 15% of the total amount invested.[55]

Leverage

Leverage Drawdown

A SBIC applies to the SBA for financial assistance (leverage) to secure the "SBA's conditional commitment to reserve a specific amount of leverage" for the SBIC's future use.[56] If the application is approved, a SBIC draws down the leverage as it makes financial commitments.

The SBA accepts draw applications from SBICs twice a month. When the draw is approved by the SBA, it issues a payment voucher to a SBIC (called an approval notice). The payment voucher has a term of approximately 60 days and provides a SBIC with the ability to draw funds on a daily basis.

A debenture is executed in conjunction with each draw and is held by an agent of a bank selected by the SBA (Federal Home Loan Bank of Chicago), which provides interim funding to the SBIC until a "SBIC's debenture(s) can be pooled with others and sold to the public, a process that occurs every six months [each March and September]."[57] During the interim period, the bank charges a SBIC the London Interbank Offered Rate (LIBOR), plus a 30 basis point premium.[58]

The SBA determines the size of the debenture pool two weeks prior to each scheduled pooling date. All of "the debentures scheduled to be pooled are purchased and pooled together by an entity called the Investment Trust which is managed by the Bank of New York Mellon" and, as the pooling occurs, "the SBA signs an agreement with the Trust to guarantee all the interest and principal payments due on each of the debentures in the pool."[59] The trust then securitizes the pool of debentures and issues new securities called trust certificates. Underwriters are hired to sell the trust certificates to investors in the public market. An offering circular is issued to notify

---

[54] U.S. Small Business Administration, "For SBICs: Background Information on Low or Moderate Income (LMI) Debentures," at http://www.sba.gov/content/low-or-moderate-income-lmi-debentures.

[55] U.S. Small Business Administration, "SBIC Program Licensees Financing to Small Businesses Reported Between October 2011 and September 2012."

[56] 13 CFR §107.1100.

[57] U.S. Small Business Administration, "Funding the SBIC Program: An Overview," at http://www.sba.gov/content/funding-sbic-program-overview. The SBA is required by statute to issue guarantees "at periodic intervals of not less than every 12 months and shall do so at such shorter intervals as it deems appropriate, taking into consideration the amount and number of such guarantees or trust certificates." See 15 U.S.C. §687m.

[58] U.S. Small Business Administration, "Funding the SBIC Program: An Overview," at http://www.sba.gov/content/funding-sbic-program-overview.

[59] Ibid.

---

investors of the trust certificates' availability, the terms of the securities, and information concerning how they can be purchased.[60]

The SBA operates the SBIC program on a zero-subsidy basis. To recoup its expenses should defaults occur, the SBA is authorized to charge SBICs a 3% origination fee for each debenture and for each participating security issued (1% at commitment and 2% at draw), an annual fee (not to exceed 1.38% for debentures and 1.46% for participating securities) on the leverage drawn, which is fixed at the time of the leverage commitment, and other administrative and underwriting fees which are adjusted annually.[61]

Debenture SBIC Leverage Requirements

A licensed debenture SBIC in good standing, with a demonstrated need for funds, may apply to the SBA for financial assistance (leverage) of up to 300% of its private capital. However, the SBA has traditionally approved debenture SBICs for a maximum of 200% of their private capital and no fund management team may exceed the allowable maximum amount of leverage of $150 million per SBIC and $225 million for two or more licenses under common control.[62] A SBIC licensed on or after October 1, 2009, may elect to have a maximum leverage amount of $175 million per SBIC and $250 million for two or more licenses under common control if it has invested at least 50% of its financings in low-income geographic areas and certifies that at least 50% of its future investments will be in low-income geographic areas.[63]

Debenture SBICs obtain leverage from the sale of SBA-guaranteed debenture participation trust certificates. SBA-guaranteed debenture participation trust certificates may have a term of up to 15 years, although only one outstanding SBA-guaranteed debenture participation trust certificate has a term exceeding 10 years and all recent public offerings have specified a term of 10 years.[64] Debenture SBICs are required to make semi-annual payments on the interest due on the debenture, semi-annual payments on the SBA's annual charge, and a lump sum principal payment

---

[60] To view recent SBIC debenture offering circulars see U.S. Small Business Administration, "SBIC Debentures Offering Circulars," at http://www.sba.gov/category/lender-navigation/sba-loan-programs/sbic-program/program-data-performance/information-tru-1.

[61] 13 CFR §107.1130; and 13 CFR §107.1210.

[62] 13 CFR §107.1120; 13 CFR §107.1150; and U.S. Small Business Administration, "American Recovery and Reinvestment Act of 2009: Implementation of SBIC Program Changes," letter from Harry Haskins, Acting Associate Administrator for Investment, to All Small Business Investment Companies (SBICs) and Applicants, May 4, 2009, p. 1, at http://archive.sba.gov/idc/groups/public/documents/sba_program_office/inv_rcvry_act_sbic_changes.pdf.

[63] 13 CFR §107.1150. A low-income area is (1) any population census tract that has a poverty rate that is not less than 20% or (a) if located within a metropolitan area, 50% or more of the households in that census tract have an income equal to less than 60% of the area median gross income; or (b) if not located within a metropolitan area, the median household income in that census tract does not exceed 80% of the statewide median household income; or (c) has been determined by the SBA Administrator to contain a substantial population of low-income individuals in residence, an inadequate access to investment capital, or other indications of economic distress; or (2) any area located within (i) a Historically Underutilized Business Zone; (ii) an Urban Empowerment Zone or Urban Enterprise Community (as designated by the Secretary of the United States Department of Housing and Urban Development); or (iii) a Rural Empowerment Zone or Rural Enterprise Community (as designated by the Secretary of the United States Department of Agriculture). See 13 CFR §108.50.

[64] One debenture has a term of 10 years and 29 weeks. See U.S. Small Business Administration, "Offering Circular, Guaranteed 2.245% Debenture Participating Securities, Series SBIC 2012-10B," September 11, 2012, at http://www.sba.gov/content/sbic-2012-10-b-cusip-831641-ex9.

---

to investors at maturity.[65] SBICs are allowed to prepay SBA-guaranteed debentures without penalty. However, a SBA-guaranteed debenture must be prepaid in whole and not in part, and can only be prepaid on a semi-annual payment date. The debenture's coupon (interest) rate is determined by market conditions and the interest rate of 10-year treasury securities at the time of the sale.[66] Also, as mentioned previously, LMI debentures are available in two maturities, for five years and 10 years (plus the stub period).

Because the SBA guarantees the debenture, investors are more likely to purchase a debenture participation trust certificate as opposed to others available on the market. They are also more likely to accept a lower coupon (interest) rate than what would be expected without the SBA's guarantee.[67] As a result, the SBIC program enhances a SBIC's access to venture capital, and reduces its cost of raising additional financial resources.

Because debenture SBICs are required to make semi-annual interest payments on the debenture and semi-annual payments on the SBA's annual charge, they tend to focus their investments on mid- and later-stage small businesses that have a positive cash flow. Businesses with a positive cash flow have resources available to make payments to the debenture SBIC, either in the form of interest payments or dividends. In many instances, small businesses with positive cash flow are seeking capital for expansion.[68]

Participating Securities SBIC Leverage Requirements

Although the SBA is no longer issuing new commitments for participating securities, the SBA is authorized to accept an application from a licensed participating securities SBIC for leverage of up to 200% of its private capital.[69] Also, no fund management team may exceed the allowable maximum amount of leverage of $150 million per SBIC and $225 million for two or more licenses under common control.

Participating securities SBICs obtained leverage by issuing SBA-guaranteed participating securities. The SBA pooled these participating securities and sold SBA-guaranteed participating securities certificates, representing an undivided interest in the pool, to investors through periodic

---

[65] U.S. Small Business Administration, "Small Business Investment Companies (SBICs)," *Small Business Notes*, 2009, at http://www.smallbusinessnotes.com/business-finances/small-business-investment-companies-sbics.html; and U.S. Small Business Administration, "For SBIC Applicants: Financing Options Explained," at http://www.sba.gov/content/financing-options-explained.

[66] Ibid.; 13 CFR §107.50; and 13 CFR §107.1150.

[67] The coupon (interest) rate on SBA debentures is based on the 10-year Treasury rate (adjusted to the nearest 1/8th of one percent) plus a market-driven spread, currently about 70-90 basis points. See 13 CFR §107.50; and U.S. Small Business Administration, "Trust Certificate Rates: SBIC Debenture Pools," at http://www.sba.gov/content/trust-certificate-rates-sbic-debenture-poolsat http://archive.sba.gov/aboutsba/sbaprograms/inv/faq/index.html. The coupon rate for the most recent sale of a SBA debenture participating certificate, which took place on September 11, 2012, was 2.245%. See U.S. Small Business Administration, "Offering Circular, Guaranteed 2.245% Debenture Participating Securities, Series SBIC 2012-10B," September 11, 2012, at http://www.sba.gov/content/sbic-2012-10-b-cusip-831641-ex9.

[68] U.S. Congress, House Committee on Small Business, Small Business Financing and Investment Act of 2009, report to accompany H.R. 3854, 111th Cong., 1st sess., October 26, 2009, H.Rept. 111-315 (Washington: GPO, 2009), p. 11; and U.S. Small Business Administration, "SBIC Program: FAQs: 8. What investment styles and fund types fit best with the SBIC Program?" at http://www.sba.gov/content/faqs.

[69] 13 CFR §107.1170.

---

public offerings. SBA participating securities may have a term of up to 15 years, but all recent public offerings had a specified a term of 10 years.

There were 35 public offerings of SBA-guaranteed participating securities certificates since the start of the participating securities program, amounting to just under $10.3 billion. The final SBA-guaranteed participating securities certificate, for $332 million, had a term of 10 years and was offered to investors on February 19, 2009, with delivery of the certificates on February 25, 2009.[70]

SBIC participating securities certificates provide for quarterly payments to investors from dividends on preferred stock, interest on an income bond, or a priority return on a preferred limited partnership equal to a specified interest rate on the principal amount and a lump sum principal payment at maturity. A participating securities SBIC is obligated to make these quarterly payments "only to the extent it has sufficient profits available to make such payments."[71] If a participating securities SBIC is unable to make any required payment, the SBA will make the payment on its behalf. Because startup and early stage small businesses often are not initially profitable, the SBA included language in its participating securities' offering circulars that it "anticipates that it will be called upon routinely to make such … payments for the SBICs in the early years of the lives of such SBICs" and that it "expects to be reimbursed [by the SBIC] any amounts paid … under its guarantee over the life of a participating security."[72]

Because the SBA guaranteed the certificate, investors were more likely to purchase a SBIC participating securities certificate as opposed to others available on the market. They were also more likely to accept a lower payment rate than what would be expected without the SBA's guarantee.[73]

In addition, participating securities SBICs are more likely than debenture SBICs to invest in startup and early stage small businesses because the SBA is willing to make a participating securities SBIC's required quarterly payments to investors, at least during the early years of the investment. Because participating securities SBICs are not required to make these quarterly payments, they are encouraged to focus on a small business's long-term prospects for growth and profitability, rather than on its prospects for having immediate, positive cash-flow.[74]

---

[70] 13 CFR §107.1500; and U.S. Small Business Administration, "Offering Circular, Guaranteed 4.727% Participating Securities Participation Certificates, Series SBIC-PS 2009-10 A," February 19, 2009, pp. 7, 14, at http://www.sba.gov/content/sbic-ps-2009-10-cusip-831641-ep6.

[71] U.S. Small Business Administration, "Offering Circular, Guaranteed 4.727% Participating Securities Participation Certificates, Series SBIC-PS 2009-10 A," February 19, 2009, p. 2, at http://www.sba.gov/content/sbic-ps-2009-10-cusip-831641-ep6.

[72] Ibid., pp. 2, 3. Also, see U.S. Congress, House Committee on Small Business, *Private Equity for Small Firms: The Importance of the Participating Securities Program*, 109th Cong., 1st sess., April 13, 2005, Serial No. 109-10 (Washington: GPO, 2005), p. 5.

[73] The coupon rate for most recent sale of a SBA guaranteed participating securities participation certificate, which took place on February 25, 2009, was 4.727%. U.S. Small Business Administration, "Offering Circular, Guaranteed 4.727% Participating Securities Participation Certificates, Series SBIC-PS 2009-10 A," February 19, 2009, p. 1, at http://www.sba.gov/content/sbic-ps-2009-10-cusip-831641-ep6.

[74] U.S. Congress, House Committee on Small Business, Small Business Financing and Investment Act of 2009, report to accompany H.R. 3854, 111th Cong., 1st sess., October 26, 2009, H.Rept. 111-315 (Washington: GPO, 2009), p. 11; and U.S. Small Business Administration, "SBIC Program: FAQs 7. What is the status of the Participating Securities Program?" at http://www.sba.gov/content/faqs.

As of September 30, 2012, the SBA had a guarantee on an outstanding unpaid principal balance of $4.9 billion in SBIC debentures, $1.5 billion in SBIC participating securities, and $15.9 million in SSBIC financings.[75] The SBA also had an outstanding commitment on $2.4 billion in SBIC debentures and $24.8 million in outstanding SBIC participating securities.[76]

Impact Investment Debenture SBIC Leverage Requirements

On April 7, 2011, the SBA announced that it was establishing a $1 billion Impact Investment SBIC Initiative (up to $150 million in leverage in FY2012, and up to $200 million in leverage per fiscal year thereafter until the limit is reached). SBA licensed impact investment debenture SBICs are required to invest at least 50% of their investments, "which target areas of critical national priority including underserved markets and communities facing barriers to access to credit and capital."[77] On July 26, 2011, the SBA announced that the first impact investment debenture SBIC license was awarded to InvestMichigan! Mezzanine Fund.[78]

Licensed impact investment debenture SBICs may apply to the SBA for leverage of up to 300% of its private capital, limited to $80 million. In addition, they may receive leverage amounting to no more than 100% of their private capital during any fiscal year (subject to the $80 million limit and the availability of impact investment initiative financing). It is anticipated that the SBA will limit impact investment debenture SBICs to a maximum of 200% of their private capital, up to $80 million.[79]

Impact investment debenture SBICs obtain leverage in the same way that debenture SBICs obtain leverage — through the issuance of SBA-guaranteed debentures with a term of up to 10 years. They are also subject to the same terms and conditions as debenture SBICs, except they are provided an expedited application review process.

Early Stage Debenture SBIC Leverage Requirements

On April 27, 2012, the SBA published a final rule in the *Federal Register* establishing the $1 billion Early Stage Innovation SBIC Initiative (up to $150 million in SBA leverage in FY2012, and up to $200 million in SBA leverage per fiscal year thereafter until the limit is reached). A licensed early stage SBIC may apply to the SBA for leverage of up to 100% of its private capital, limited to $50 million. The SBA does not consider applications from an early stage SBIC applicant that is under common control with another early stage SBIC applicant or an existing

---

[75] U.S. Small Business Administration, Investment Division, "SBIC Program Overview," September 30, 2012.

[76] Ibid.

[77] U.S. Small Business Administration, "Impact Investment Initiative," at http://www.sba.gov/content/small-business-investment-company-sbic-impact-investment-initiative-2.

[78] U.S. Small Business Administration, "SBA Licenses First Impact Investment Fund in Michigan," July 26, 2011, at http://www.sba.gov/content/sba-licenses-first-impact-investment-fund-michigan. Mezzanine financing is a hybrid of debt and equity financing and is typically used to finance the expansion of an existing business. It provides the lender the right to convert to an ownership or equity interest in the company if the loan is not paid back in time and in full. It is generally subordinated to debt provided by senior lenders such as banks and venture capital companies.

[79] U.S. Small Business Administration, "Impact Investment Initiative," at http://www.sba.gov/content/small-business-investment-company-sbic-impact-investment-initiative-2.

early stage SBIC (unless the existing early stage SBIC has no outstanding leverage or leverage commitments and will not seek additional leverage in the future).[80]

Early stage debenture SBICs obtain leverage in the same way that debenture SBICs obtain leverage — through the issuance of SBA-guaranteed debentures with a term of up to 10 years. However, early stage debentures come in two forms: early stage standard debentures and early stage discounted debentures.

Early stage standard SBIC debentures are similar to standard SBIC debentures, but, instead of requiring semi-annual payments on the debenture's interest and on the SBA's annual charge, they require quarterly payments on the debenture's interest and on the SBA's annual charge. In addition, early stage SBICs must maintain a reserve sufficient to pay the interest on the debenture and on the SBA's annual charges for the first 21 payment dates following the date of issuance (five years plus the stub period —the length of time between the issue date and the next March 1, June 1, September 1, or December 1).[81] Because early stage standard debentures require early stage debenture SBICs to make quarterly payments, they are most appropriate for investments in small businesses that have established a positive cash flow that enables them to pay interest or dividends to the early stage debenture SBIC.

Early stage discounted debentures are issued at a discount (less than face value) equal to the first five years' of interest on the debenture and the first five years of annual SBA charges. The discount eliminates the need for early stage debenture SBICs to make interest payments on the debenture and to make payments on the SBA's annual charge for five years from the date of issuance, plus the stub period.[82] Early stage debenture SBICs make quarterly payments on the debenture's interest and on the SBA's annual charge during years six through 10. They are also responsible for paying the debenture's principal amount when the debenture reaches its maturity date.

Because early stage discounted debentures do not require interest payments or payments on the SBA's annual charge for five years, they are most appropriate for investments in small businesses that have not established a positive cash flow to pay interest or dividends to the early stage debenture SBIC. As a result, early stage discounted debentures are designed to encourage investments in early stage small businesses, which by definition have not established a positive cash flow.

Reporting Requirements

Once licensed, each SBIC is required to file with the SBA an annual financial report that includes an audit by an SBA-approved independent public accountant. SBICs are also subject to annual onsite regulatory compliance examinations.[83] SBICs are also required to provide the SBA:

---

[80] U.S. Small Business Administration, "Small Business Investment Companies - Early Stage SBICs," 77 *Federal Register* 25052, April 27, 2012.

[81] 13 CFR §107.1181. The required reserve is reduced on each payment date upon payment of the required interest and charges.

[82] U.S. Small Business Administration, Office of Congressional and Legislative Affairs, "Correspondence with the author," May 2, 2012.

[83] 13 CFR §107.630; and 13 CFR §107.690.

- a portfolio financing report within 30 days of the closing date for each financing of a small business;[84]

- the value of its loans and investments within 90 days of the end of the fiscal year in the case of annual valuations, and within 30 days following the close of other reporting periods;[85]

- any material adverse changes in valuations at least quarterly (within 30 days following the close of the quarter);[86] and

- copies of reports provided to investors, documents filed with the Securities and Exchange Commission, and documents pertaining to litigation or other legal proceedings, including criminal charges against any person who was required by the SBA complete a personal history statement in connection with the SBIC's license.[87]

SBIC Program Statistics

At the end of FY2012, there were 301 licensed SBICs in operation (158 debenture SBICs, 86 participating securities SBICs, 44 bank-owned/non-leveraged SBICs, and 13 SSBICs).[88] In FY2012, 221 SBICs provided at least one new financing to a small business.[89]

Until this year, the number of licensed SBICs had declined each year since FY2006, with most of the decline due to the planned phase-out of participating securities SBICs and SSBICs.[90] In FY2006, there were 396 licensed SBICs (132 debenture SBICs, 173 participating securities SBICs, 67 bank-owned/non-leveraged SBICs, and 24 SSBICs).[91] There were 369 licensed SBICs in FY2007, 348 in FY2008, 315 in FY2009, 307 in FY2010, and 299 in FY2011. The SBA has made it a goal to increase the number of new SBIC licenses issued each year "to position the program for continued growth."[92]

---

[84] 13 CFR §107.640.

[85] 13 CFR §107.650.

[86] Ibid.

[87] 13 CFR §107.660.

[88] U.S. Small Business Administration, Investment Division, "SBIC Program Overview," September 30, 2012.

[89] U.S. Small Business Administration, "SBIC Program Licensees Financing to Small Businesses Reported Between October 2011 and September 2012."

[90] U.S. Small Business Administration, Investment Division, "SBIC Program Overview," September 29, 2010; and U.S. Small Business Administration, Investment Division, "SBIC Program Overview," September 30, 2012.

[91] U.S. Small Business Administration, Investment Division, "SBIC Program Overview," September 29, 2010.

[92] U.S. Small Business Administration, "FY 2012 Congressional Budget Justification and FY 2010 Annual Performance Report," p. 60, at http://www.sba.gov/sites/default/files/ FINAL%20FY%202012%20CBJ%20FY%202010%20APR_0.pdf. The SBA issued six new SBIC licenses (five to debenture SBICs and one to a bank-owned/non-leveraged SBIC) in FY2008 and 11 new SBIC licenses (eight to debenture SBICs and three to bank-owned/non-leveraged SBICs) in FY2009. The SBA issued 23 new SBIC licenses (21 to debenture SBICs and 2 to bank-owned/non-leveraged SBICs) in FY2010 and 22 new SBIC licenses (18 to debenture SBICs and 4 to bank-owned/non-leveraged SBICs) in FY2011. In FY2012, the SBA issued 30 new SBIC licenses (27 to debenture SBICs and 3 to bank-owned/non-leveraged SBICs).

Overall, SBICs pursue investments in a broad range of industries, geographic areas, and stage of investment. Some individual SBICs specialize in a particular field or industry in which their management has expertise, while others invest more generally. Most SBICs concentrate on a particular stage of investment (i.e., start-up, expansion, or turnaround) and identify a geographic area in which to focus.

Total Financing

Since its inception, the SBIC program has provided more than $62.6 billion in financial assistance and made more than 164,000 investments in small businesses.[93] As mentioned previously, as of September 30, 2012, the SBA had a guarantee on an outstanding unpaid principal balance of $4.9 billion in SBIC debentures, $1.5 billion in SBIC participating securities, and $15.9 million in SSBIC financings.[94] The SBA also had an outstanding commitment on $2.4 billion in SBIC debentures and $24.8 million in outstanding SBIC participating securities.[95] Including private investment, the SBIC program has invested or committed about $18.2 billion in small businesses, with the SBA's share of capital at risk about $8.8 billion.[96]

In FY2012, SBICs made 1,907 financings (including 58 financings by SSBICs). The average financing amount was $1,692,412 ($1,741,923 for debenture SBICs, $285,257 for participating securities SBICs, $878,299 for bank-owned/non-leveraged SBICs, and $114,053 for SSBICs).[97] The funds were used primarily for acquiring an existing business (58.1%). Other uses were for operating capital (21.7%), refinancing or refunding debt (10.1%), a new building or plant construction (1.8%), purchasing equipment (1.6%), research and development (1.3%), marketing activities (0.6%), plant modernization (0.4%), and other uses (4.4%).[98]

As shown in **Table 2**, the total amount of SBIC financing declined during the recession (December 2007-June 2009), reached pre-recession levels in FY2011, and exceeded pre-recession levels in FY2012. In FY2012, the SBA committed to guarantee $1.9 billion in SBIC small business investments and SBICs provided another $1.3 billion in investments from private capital, for a total of more than $3.2 billion in financing for 1,094 small businesses.

In addition, as shown in **Table 2**, the amount of SBA leverage as a share of total financing provided has increased in recent years. For example, the SBA's leverage commitments accounted for 12.3% of total financing in FY2005, compared with 59.6% in FY2012.

---

[93] U.S. Small Business Administration, "Offering Circular, Guaranteed 2.245% Debenture Participating Securities, Series SBIC 2012-10B," September 11, 2012, at http://www.sba.gov/content/sbic-2012-10-b-cusip-831641-ex9. The SBA has a selected list of firms that have received SBIC financing, including Apple Computer, Compaq Computer, Costco Wholesale Corporation, FedEx, Intel, Jenny Craig, Inc., Outback Steakhouse, Sports Authority, Staples, and Sun Microsystems, on its website. See U.S. Small Business Administration, "Investment Division," at http://archive.sba.gov/aboutsba/sbaprograms/inv/INV_SUCCESS_STORIES.html.

[94] U.S. Small Business Administration, Investment Division, "SBIC Program Overview," September 30, 2012.

[95] Ibid.

[96] Ibid.

[97] U.S. Small Business Administration, "SBIC Program Licensees Financing to Small Businesses Reported Between October 2011 and September 2012."

[98] Ibid.

The SBA has had congressional authorization to issue up to $3.0 billion in SBIC leverage each year since 2005. For comparative purposes, private venture capital firms invested $20.2 billion in 3,110 companies in 2009, $23.4 billion in 3,598 companies in 2010, and $29.5 billion in 3,838 companies in 2011. As of September 30, 2012, private venture capital firms were on pace to invest $26.7 billion in 3,556 companies in 2012.[99]

Table 2. SBIC Investments, FY2005-FY2012

($ in millions)

Year	SBA Leverage/Guarantee Commitments	Private-Sector Investment	Total Financing	# of Small Businesses Financed
FY2012	$1,924	$1,303	$3,227	1,094
FY2011	$1,828	$1,005	$2,833	1,339
FY2010	$1,165	$882	$2,047	1,331
FY2009	$788	$1,068	$1,856	1,481
FY2008	$1,029	$1,398	$2,427	1,905
FY2007	$708	$1,940	$2,648	2,057
FY2006	$477	$2,420	$2,897	2,121
FY2005	$355	$2,540	$2,895	2,298

Source: U.S. Small Business Administration, "Performance and Financial Highlights, FY2007," February 4, 2008, p. 4; U.S. Small Business Administration, "FY2008 Budget Request and Performance Plan," 2007, p. 23; U.S. Small Business Administration, Investment Division, "SBIC Program Overview," January 23, 2009; U.S. Small Business Administration, "SBIC Program Overview: Program Achievements & Success Stories," at http://www.sba.gov/content/sbic-program-overview-2; and U.S. Small Business Administration, Investment Division, "SBIC Program Overview," September 30, 2012.

The SBA has indicated that one of its goals is "to enhance program acceptance in the marketplace and increase the number of funds licensed and the amount of leverage issued so as to improve capital access for small businesses."[100]

In 2008, the Urban Institute released an analysis comparing debenture SBIC investments made from 1997 to 2005 to private-sector venture capital investments made during that time period in second stage business loans, third stage business loans, and bridge loans "because these investments are likely to be of the same character (debt with equity features) as those made by debenture SBICs."[101] The Urban Institute found that debenture SBIC investments accounted for more than 62% of all venture capital financings in second stage business loans, third stage business loans, and bridge loans in the United States during that time period. However, because

---

[99] National Venture Capital Association, "Corporate VC Stats as of 9/30/2012," Arlington, VA, at http://www.nvca.org/index.php?option=com_docman&task=cat_view&gid=99&Itemid=317.

[100] U.S. Small Business Administration, "Fiscal Year 2011 Congressional Budget Justification and FY2009 Annual Performance Report," p. 52.

[101] Kenneth Temkin and Brett Theodos, with Kerstin Gentsch, "The Debenture Small Business Investment Company Program: A Comparative Analysis of Investment Patterns with Private Venture Capital Equity," Washington, DC: The Urban Institute, January 2008, p. 3, at http://www.urban.org/UploadedPDF/411601_sbic_gap_analysis.pdf.

the average amount of an SBIC debenture investment was much smaller than the industry average, SBIC debenture investments accounted for "only 8% of total dollars invested."[102]

Financing to Specific Demographic Groups

As shown in **Table 3**, in FY2012, SBICs made 116 financings (6.1% of all financings) amounting to $128.1 million (4.0% of the total amount of financings) to minority-owned and -controlled small businesses.

Table 3. SBIC Financing, Minority-Owned Small Businesses, FY2012

Small Business Ownership Demographic	# of Financings	% of Financings	$ Amount of Financings	% of Total $ Amount of Financings
Black-Owned	42	2.2%	$56,200,200	1.7%
Subcontinent Asian-Owned	39	2.0%	$3,418,560	0.1%
Hispanic-Owned	18	0.9%	$27,987,568	0.9%
Asian Pacific-Owned	17	0.9%	$40,490,376	1.3%
Native American-Owned	0	0.0%	$0	0.0%
Subtotal	116	6.1%	$128,096,704	4.0%
Other (non-minority)	1,791	93.9%	$3,099,333,671	96.0%
Total—All Financings	1,907	100.0%	$3,227,430,375	100.0%

Source: U.S. Small Business Administration, "SBIC Program Licensees Financing to Small Businesses Reported Between October 2011 and September 2012."

Notes: Ownership is defined as owning at least 50% of the small business.

In addition, in FY2012, SBICs made 50 financings (2.6% of all financings) amounting to $38.4 million (1.2% of the total amount of financings) to women-owned small businesses, and 9 financings (0.5% of all financings) amounting to $8.9 million (0.3% of the total amount of financings) to veteran-owned small businesses.[103]

Research concerning private venture capital investment in minority-owned or women-owned small businesses is limited. As a result, it is difficult to find the data necessary to compare the SBIC program's investment in minority-owned or women-owned small businesses to the private sector's investment in these firms.[104]

In 2007, the SBA acknowledged at a congressional hearing on the SBA's investment programs that "women and minority representation in [the SBIC program] is low" and has been low for

---

[102] Ibid., p. 1.

[103] U.S. Small Business Administration, "SBIC Program Licensees Financing to Small Businesses Reported Between October 2011 and September 2012."

[104] Kenneth Temkin and Brett Theodos, with Kerstin Gentsch, "The Debenture Small Business Investment Company Program: A Comparative Analysis of Investment Patterns with Private Venture Capital Equity," Washington, DC: The Urban Institute, January 2008, pp. 2, 26, at http://www.urban.org/UploadedPDF/411601_sbic_gap_analysis.pdf.

many years.[105] The SBA reported at that time that it did not control the investments made by SBICs, but it has tried to increase women and minority representation in the SBIC program by reaching out to venture capital firms, trade organizations, and others to better understand why women and minority representation in the SBIC program is low, and by "finding debenture firms with minority representation on their investment committees and in senior management."[106] However, despite these efforts, in 2009, the Small Business Investor Alliance (then called the National Association of Small Business Investment Companies) asserted at a congressional hearing on the SBA's capital access programs that the SBA's SBIC licensing process "has done an abysmal job at attracting and licensing funds led by women and minorities."[107]

During the 111th Congress, S. 1831, the Small Business Venture Capital Act of 2009, was introduced on October 21, 2009, and referred to the Senate Committee on Small Business and Entrepreneurship. No further action was taken on the bill. It would have encouraged SBIC investments in women-owned small businesses and socially and economically disadvantaged small business concerns by increasing the amount of leverage available to SBICs that invest at least 50% of their financings in small business concerns owned and controlled by women or socially and economically disadvantaged small business concerns.

Financing by State

As shown in **Table 4**, in FY2012, SBICs provided financing to small businesses located in 45 states, the District of Columbia, and Puerto Rico, with the most financings taking place in California (247 financings amounting to $480.1 million), New York (226 financings amounting to $261.8 million), and Texas (182 financings amounting to $348.6 million).

Table 4. SBIC Financing, by State, FY2012

($ in millions)

State	# of Financings	Amount of Financings	State	# of Financings	Amount of Financings
Alabama	5	$34.2	Montana	0	$0.0
Alaska	0	$0.0	Nebraska	0	$0.0
Arizona	14	$27.7	Nevada	2	$0.8
Arkansas	10	$2.4	New Hampshire	10	$1.4
California	247	$480.1	New Jersey	120	$149.1
Colorado	36	$62.6	New Mexico	13	$12.9
Connecticut	24	$50.8	New York	226	$261.8
Delaware	7	$1.4	North Carolina	33	$96.4

[105] U.S. Congress, House Committee on Small Business, *Full Committee Hearing on Legislation Updating and Improving the SBA's Investment and Surety Bond Programs*, 110th Cong., 1st sess., September 6, 2007, Serial Number 110-44 (Washington: GPO, 2007), p. 15.

[106] Ibid.

[107] U.S. Congress, House Committee on Small Business, *Full Committee Hearing On Increasing Capital For Small Business*, 111th Cong., 1st sess., October 14, 2009, House Small Business Committee Document No. 111-051 (Washington: GPO, 2009), p. 89.

State	# of Financings	Amount of Financings	State	# of Financings	Amount of Financings
District of Columbia	9	$15.6	North Dakota	1	$1.5
Florida	100	$179.2	Ohio	36	$59.6
Georgia	46	$135.0	Oklahoma	20	$15.6
Hawaii	1	$2.5	Oregon	15	$36.4
Idaho	2	$.2	Pennsylvania	67	$156.1
Illinois	108	$189.9	Puerto Rico	3	$13.4
Indiana	18	$46.1	Rhode Island	3	$4.0
Iowa	9	$20.4	South Carolina	16	$10.9
Kansas	26	$17.3	South Dakota	0	$0.0
Kentucky	12	$48.1	Tennessee	36	$78.1
Louisiana	11	$24.3	Texas	182	$348.6
Maine	1	$9.7	Utah	72	$39.2
Maryland	15	$52.5	Vermont	5	$13.2
Massachusetts	143	$125.2	Virginia	65	$79.2
Michigan	24	$80.0	Washington	25	$22.9
Minnesota	35	$110.3	West Virginia	2	$10.8
Mississippi	17	$1.7	Wisconsin	19	$70.8
Missouri	16	$27.4	Wyoming	0	$0.0
Total				1,907	$3,227.4

Source: U.S. Small Business Administration, "SBIC Program Licensees Financing to Small Businesses Reported Between October 2011 and September 2012."

The previously mentioned 2008 Urban Institute comparative analysis of debenture SBIC financing from 1997 to 2005 found that the dollar volume of investments from debenture SBICs was more evenly distributed across the nation than from comparable private venture capital funds. For example, the Urban Institute found that California (45.8%) and Massachusetts (12.9%) received the largest share of the total dollar volume invested by private venture capital funds from 1997 to 2005. The two states accounted for more than half (58.7%) of the total dollar volume invested by private venture capital funds. In contrast, New York (18.7%) and California (11.1%) received the largest share of the total dollar volume invested by debenture SBICs from 1997 to 2005. The two states accounted for less than one-third (29.8%) of the total dollar volume invested by debenture SBICs. Also, the top 10 states in terms of their share of the total dollar volume invested accounted nearly 84% of the total invested by private venture capital funds, compared with 64% for debenture SBICs.[108]

A comparison of the state-by-state distribution of private-sector venture capital fund investments and SBIC financings in FY2012 (see **Table 4**) suggest that the Urban Institute's finding that

---

[108] Kenneth Temkin and Brett Theodos, with Kerstin Gentsch, "The Debenture Small Business Investment Company Program: A Comparative Analysis of Investment Patterns with Private Venture Capital Equity," Washington, DC: The Urban Institute, January 2008, pp. 3, 18-24, at http://www.urban.org/UploadedPDF/411601_sbic_gap_analysis.pdf.

SBICs investments were more evenly distributed across the nation than private-sector venture capital fund investments from 1997 to 2005 continue to be the case today.[109] For example, California (53.7%), Massachusetts (11.6%), New York (6.4%), and Texas (3.6%) received the largest share of the total dollar volume invested by private venture capital funds during the first three quarters of FY2012. The four states accounted for about three-quarters (75.3%) of the total dollar volume invested by private venture capital funds. In contrast, the four states with the largest share of the total volume invested by SBICs in FY2012 (California at 14.9%, Texas at 10.8%, New York at 8.1%, and Illinois at 5.9%) accounted for 39.7% of the total dollar volume invested by SBICs.

Financing by Industry

As shown on **Table 5**, in FY2012, SBIC financings were made in a variety of industries, led by investments in manufacturing; professional, scientific, and technical services; transportation and warehousing; and information.

The previously mentioned 2008 Urban Institute comparative analysis of SBIC financings from 1997 to 2005 found that "SBIC financing is less concentrated by industry than financing from private venture capital firms" and "total financings by SBICs are much less likely to be in high-tech industries" than comparable private-sector venture capital investment firms.[110] The Urban Institute found that unlike SBICs, "the value of investments by private venture capital firms is predominately directed towards information and finance," with computer and Internet firms receiving roughly half of all private-sector investments.[111]

Table 5. SBIC Financing, by Industry, FY2012

Industry	# of Financings	% of Financings	$ Amount of Financings	% of $ Amount of Financings
Manufacturing	537	28.2%	$884,493,305	27.4%
Professional, Scientific, and Technical Services	300	15.7%	$508,094,582	15.7%
Transportation and Warehousing	242	12.7%	$162,474,082	5.0%
Information	216	11.3%	$268,203,978	8.3%
Administrative and Support and Waste Management	108	5.7%	$224,893,219	7.0%
Retail Trade	93	4.9%	$161,415,213	5.0%
Wholesale Trade	91	4.8%	$214,011,523	6.6%
Accommodation and Food Services	74	3.9%	$127,083,453	3.9%
Health Care and Social Assistance	56	2.9%	$170,186,509	5.3%

[109] National Venture Capital Association, "Venture Capital Investments Q3-2012 – MoneyTree Results, Regional Data," Arlington, VA, at http://www.nvca.org/.

[110] Kenneth Temkin and Brett Theodos, with Kerstin Gentsch, "The Debenture Small Business Investment Company Program: A Comparative Analysis of Investment Patterns with Private Venture Capital Equity," Washington, DC: The Urban Institute, January 2008, pp. 3, 11-17, at http://www.urban.org/UploadedPDF/411601_sbic_gap_analysis.pdf.

[111] Ibid., p. 11.

Industry	# of Financings	% of Financings	$ Amount of Financings	% of $ Amount of Financings
Construction	44	2.3%	$133,990,273	4.2%
Real Estate and Rental Leasing	30	1.6%	$34,340,426	1.1%
Finance and Insurance	21	1.1%	$40,144,640	1.2%
Mining	20	1.0%	$61,968,243	1.9%
Educational Services	17	0.9%	$47,601,840	1.5%
Arts, Entertainment and Recreation	14	0.7%	$28,383,083	0.9%
Management of Companies and Enterprises	5	0.3%	$44,265,110	1.4%
Other Industries	39	2.0%	$115,880,896	3.6%
Total	1,907	100.0%	$3,227,430,375	100.0%

Source: U.S. Small Business Administration, "SBIC Program Licensees Financing to Small Businesses Reported Between October 2011 and September 2012."

Legislative Activity

P.L. 111-5, the American Recovery and Reinvestment Act of 2009 (ARRA), included provisions designed to increase the amount of leverage issued under the SBIC program by increasing the maximum amount of leverage available to an individual SBIC to 300% of its private capital, or $150 million, whichever is less; and by increasing the maximum amount of leverage available for two or more licenses under common control to $225 million.[112] It also encouraged SBIC investment in smaller enterprises by requiring SBICs licensed on or after the date of its enactment (February 17, 2009) to certify that at least 25% of all future financing dollars are invested in smaller enterprises. ARRA defined smaller enterprises as firms having either a net worth of no more than $6 million and average after-tax net income for the preceding two years of no more than $2 million, or meeting the SBA's size standard for its industry classification.[113]

ARRA also encouraged SBIC investments in low-income areas by allowing a SBIC licensed on or after October 1, 2009, to elect to have a maximum leverage amount of $175 million, and $250 million for two or more licenses under common control, if the SBIC has invested at least 50% of

---

[112] 13 CFR §107.1120; 13 CFR §107.1150; and U.S. Small Business Administration, "American Recovery and Reinvestment Act of 2009: Implementation of SBIC Program Changes," letter from Harry Haskins, Acting Associate Administrator for Investment, to All Small Business Investment Companies (SBICs) and Applicants, May 4, 2009, p. 1, at http://archive.sba.gov/idc/groups/public/documents/sba_program_office/inv_rcvry_act_sbic_changes.pdf. Previously, "... the total principal amount of outstanding debentures and participating securities guaranteed by SBA and issued by any SBIC or group of commonly controlled SBICs may not, in general, exceed at any one time an amount equal to three times such SBIC's Private Capital or $130.6 million, whichever is less, of which no more than two times the SBIC's Private Capital may be represented by participating securities. Such dollar limit has been adjusted annually to reflect increases in the Consumer Price Index since March 31, 1993." See U.S. Small Business Administration, "Offering Circular, Guaranteed 5.725% Debenture Participation Certificates, Series SBIC 2008-10 B," September 18, 2008, at http://www.sba.gov/content/sbic-2008-10-b-cusip-831641-en1.

[113] 13 CFR §107.1150; and 13 CFR §107.710.

its financings in low-income geographic areas and certified that at least 50% of its future investments will be in low-income geographic areas.[114]

As part of its Startup America Initiative, on January 31, 2012, the Obama Administration recommended that the SBIC program's annual authorization be increased to $4 billion from $3 billion and that the amount of SBA leverage available to licensees under common control be increased to $350 million from $225 million.[115] As will be discussed, several bills were subsequently introduced during the 112th Congresses to either target additional leverage to startup companies or to expand the program.

Legislation to Target Additional Assistance to Startup and Early Stage Small Businesses

As mentioned previously, some Members and small business advocates have proposed that the SBIC program target additional assistance to startup and early stage small businesses, which are generally viewed as relatively risky investments but also as having a relatively high potential for job creation. Advocates of targeting additional assistance to startup and early stage small businesses argue that the SBA's participating securities program was created to fill a perceived investment gap resulting from the SBA's debenture program's focus on mid- and later-stage small businesses. Because the SBA is no longer providing new licenses or leverage for participating securities SBICs, several Members have introduced legislation to create a new SBA program that would focus on the investment needs of startup and early stage small businesses.

For example, during the 111th Congress the House passed, by a vote of 241-182, H.R. 5297, the Small Business Jobs and Credit Act of 2010.[116] Among its provisions, as passed by the House, H.R. 5297 would have authorized a $1 billion Small Business Early Stage Investment Program. The proposed program would have provided equity investment financing of up to $100 million in matching funds to each participating investment company. It would have required participating investment companies to invest in small businesses, with at least 50% of the financing in early stage small businesses, defined as those small businesses not having "gross annual sales revenues exceeding $15 million in any of the previous three years."[117] The proposed program emphasized venture capital investments in startup companies operating in nine targeted industries.[118]

H.R. 5297, as subsequently enacted by Congress and signed into law by President Obama on September 27, 2010 (P.L. 111-240, the Small Business Jobs Act of 2010) did not include

---

[114] 13 CFR §107.1150.

[115] The White House, "Startup America Legislative Agenda," January 31, 2012, at http://www.whitehouse.gov/sites/default/files/uploads/startup_america_legislative_agenda.pdf.

[116] Representative Edward Perlmutter, "Providing for Further Consideration of H.R. 5297, Small Business Jobs and Credit Act of 2010, Roll No. 368," *Congressional Record*, daily edition, vol. 156, no. 91 (June 17, 2010), pp. H4608, H 4609.

[117] H.R. 5297, the Small Business Lending Fund Act of 2010, Section 399L. Definitions.

[118] Ibid. The nine targeted industries are: agricultural technology, energy technology, environmental technology, life science, information technology, digital media, clean technology, defense technology, and photonics technology. A similar $200 million Small Business Early Stage Investment Program was included in H.R. 3854, the Small Business Financing and Investment Act of 2009, which was passed by the House on October 29, 2009, by a vote of 389-32. It is awaiting action in the Senate.

---

legislative language authorizing a Small Business Early Stage Investment Program.[119] However, it authorized a three-year Intermediary Lending Pilot Program to provide direct loans to not more than 20 eligible nonprofit lending intermediaries each year, totaling not more than $20 million and $1 million per intermediary. The intermediaries, in turn, may make loans to new or growing small businesses, not to exceed $200,000 per business.[120] On August 4, 2011, the SBA announced the selection of the first 20 lenders to participate in the program.[121]

Discussion

Advocates of efforts to encourage capital investment in startup and early stage small businesses, including Members of Congress who have served on the House or Senate Small Business Committees, have argued that the SBA's elimination of the SBIC participating securities program has created a gap "in the SBA's existing array of capital access programs, particularly in the provision of capital to early stage small businesses in capital-intensive industries."[122] As Representative Nydia Velázquez argued on the House floor during congressional consideration of H.R. 5297

> This legislation, Mr. Chairman, also recognizes that capital markets are changing dramatically. Credit standards are stricter, and small businesses are now looking not only to loans and to credit cards to finance their operations, but they are also looking to equity investment to turn their ideas into reality. This has become even more pronounced as asset values have declined, leaving entrepreneurs with less collateral to borrow against. Unfortunately, small firms' access to venture capital and to equity investment has declined. Last year, such investments plummeted from $28 billion in 2008 to only $17 billion last year. This is due, in part, to the previous administration's decision to terminate the SBA's largest pure equity financing program—the Small Business Investment Company Participating Securities program. This has left many entrepreneurs who need equity investment to fulfill their business plans without a source of such financing.[123]

Opponents of efforts to encourage capital investment in startup and early stage small businesses have argued that such efforts could "pile unnecessary risk or costs onto taxpayers at a time when we're dealing with record debt and unsustainable deficit spending."[124] During consideration of the

---

[119] Senator Al Franken, "Small Business Lending Fund Act of 2010," Rollcall Vote No. 237 Leg., *Congressional Record*, daily edition, vol. 156, part 125 (September 16, 2010), p. S7158.

[120] P.L. 111-240, the Small Business Jobs Act of 2010, Section 1131. Small Business Intermediary Lending Pilot Program.

[121] U.S. Small Business Administration, "Small Businesses Have New Non-Profit Sources for SBA-financed Loans," August 4, 2011, at http://www.sba.gov/content/intermediary-lending-pilot-program-0.

[122] U.S. Congress, House Committee on Small Business, *Small Business Financing and Investment Act of 2009*, report to accompany H.R. 3854, 111th Cong., 1st sess., October 26, 2009, H.Rept. 111-315, p. 2. For the arguments presented by various organizations advocating programs to assist early stage small businesses and startups see U.S. Congress, House Committee on Small Business, *Subcommittee on Finance and Tax Hearing on Legislative Proposals to Reform the SBA's Capital Access Programs*, 111th Cong., 1st sess., July 23, 2009, House Small Business Committee Document No. 111-039 (Washington: GPO, 2009), pp. 10-12, 60-67; and U.S. Congress, House Committee on Small Business, *Full Committee Hearing on Increasing Access to Capital for Small Business*, 111th Cong., 1st sess., October 14, 2009, House Small Business Committee Document No. 111-051 (Washington: GPO, 2009), pp. 33-35, 50-54, 63-69, 86-99.

[123] Representative Nydia Velázquez, "Small Business Jobs and Credit Act of 2010," House debate, *Congressional Record*, daily edition, vol. 156, no. 90 (June 16, 2010), p. H4516.

[124] Representative Sam Graves, "Small Business Jobs and Credit Act of 2010," House debate, *Congressional Record*, vol. 156, no. 90 (June 16, 2010), p. H4516.

---

proposed Small Business Early Stage Investment Program, opponents argued that it was untested, would likely encourage risky investments, and the legislation required "only 50% of the funding … to be invested" in early stage small businesses.[125]

Legislation to Increase SBIC Financing Levels

In 2009, the Small Business Investor Alliance characterized the SBIC program as "dramatically underused."[126] It argued that the program's financing levels would increase if (1) the SBA further improved its licensing processing procedures to make them more timely and objective, (2) the percentage of SBIC regulatory capital allowed from state or local government entities was increased from its present maximum of 33%, and (3) the SBIC program's family of funds limit ($225 million for two or more licenses under common control) was increased to allow SBICs to have a series of investment funds in place, where, for example, "one fund could be winding down, another could be at peak, and another could just be ramping up."[127]

During the 111th Congress, H.R. 3854, the Small Business Financing and Investment Act of 2009, which was passed by the House on October 29, 2009, and H.R. 5554, the Small Business Assistance and Relief Act of 2010, which was not reported after being referred to five committees for consideration, proposed to encourage greater use of the SBIC program by increasing the maximum percentage of SBIC regulatory capital allowed from state or local government entities to 45% from 33%.[128] Both measures would have also increased the SBIC program's family of funds limit to $350 million from $225 million; increased the SBIC program's limit of $250 million to $400 million for multiple funds under common control that were licensed after September 30, 2009, and invested 50% of their dollars in low-income geographic areas; and increased the SBIC program's authorization level from to $5.5 billion from $3 billion in FY2011.[129]

The Obama Administration also recommended, as part of its Startup America Initiative (which included the SBA's $1 billion early stage debenture SBIC initiative and $1 billion impact investment SBIC initiative), that the 112th Congress adopt legislation to increase the SBIC program's annual authorization to $4 billion from $3 billion. The Administration recommended as

---

[125] Ibid; and Representative Jeff Flake, "Small Business Early Stage Investment Act of 2009," House debate, *Congressional Record*, vol. 155, no. 171 (November 18, 2009), p. H13083. Note: H.R. 3738, the Small Business Early-Stage Investment Act of 2009, was one of eight bills merged into H.R. 3854, the Small Business Financing and Investment Act of 2009, and was later added to H.R. 5297, Small Business Jobs and Credit Act of 2010, by H.Res. 1436.

[126] U.S. Congress, House Committee on Small Business, *Full Committee Hearing On Increasing Capital For Small Business*, 111th Cong., 1st sess., October 14, 2009, House Small Business Committee Document No. 111-051 (Washington: GPO, 2009), pp. 32, 87.

[127] Ibid., pp. 88, 89.

[128] H.R. 3854, the Small Business Financing and Investment Act of 2009, Section 401. Increased Investment from States; and H.R. 5554, the Small Business Assistance and Relief Act of 2010, Section 591. Increased Investment from States.

[129] H.R. 3854, the Small Business Financing and Investment Act of 2009, Section 401. Increased Investment From States, Section 403. Revised Leverage Limitations For Successful SBICs, and Section 408. Program Levels; and H.R. 5554, the Small Business Assistance and Relief Act of 2010, Section 591. Increased Investment from States, Section 593. Revised Leverage Limitations for Successful SBICs, and Section 598. Program Levels.

---

well that the 112th Congress adopt legislation to increase the amount of SBA leverage available to licensees under common control to $350 million from $225 million.[130]

During the 112th Congress, H.R. 3219, the Small Business Investment Company Modernization Act of 2011, was introduced on October 14, 2011, and referred to the House Committee on Small Business. No further action has, so far, taken place on the bill. It proposes to encourage greater utilization of the SBIC program by increasing the maximum amount of outstanding SBA leverage available to any single licensed SBIC from the lesser of 300% of its private capital or $150 million, to the lesser of 300% of its private capital or $200 million if a majority of the managers of the company are experienced in managing one or more SBIC licensed companies. It would also increase the maximum amount of outstanding SBA leverage available to two or more licenses under common control to $350 million from $225 million.

S. 2136, a bill to increase the maximum amount of leverage permitted under title III of the Small Business Investment Act of 1958, was introduced on February 28, 2012, and referred to the Senate Committee on Small Business and Entrepreneurship. No further action has yet taken place on the bill. It proposes to encourage greater use of the SBIC program by increasing the maximum amount of outstanding SBA leverage available to two or more licenses under common control to $350 million from $225 million. It would also increase the SBIC program's authorization level to $4 billion from $3 billion.

On March 15, 2012, S.Amdt. 1833, the INVEST in America Act of 2012, was offered on the Senate floor as an amendment in the nature of a substitute to H.R. 3606, the Jumpstart Our Business Startups Act, which had previously passed the House. Two of the provisions in the amendment proposed to encourage greater use of the SBIC program by (1) increasing the maximum amount of outstanding SBA leverage available to two or more licenses under common control to $350 million from $225 million and (2) increasing the SBIC program's authorization level to $4 billion from $3 billion. The Senate later passed H.R. 3606 with amendments, which did not address the SBIC program. The House accepted the Senate amendments and passed the bill, which President Obama signed into law (P.L. 112-106).

S. 3442, the SUCCESS Act of 2012, which was introduced on July 25, 2012, and S. 3572, the Restoring Tax and Regulatory Certainty to Small Businesses Act of 2012, which was introduced on September 19, 2012, would, among other provisions, increase the program's authorization amount to $4 billion from $3 billion, increase the program's family of funds limit (the amount of outstanding leverage allowed for two or more SBIC licenses under common control) to $350 million from $225 million, and annually adjust the maximum outstanding leverage amount available to both individual SBICs and SBICs under common control to account for inflation. Both bills were referred to the Senate Committee on Finance. No further action has yet taken place on the bills.

Also, H.R. 6504, the Small Business Investment Company Modernization Act of 2012, was introduced on September 21, 2012 and referred to the House Committee on Small Business. It would increase the program's family of funds limit (the amount of outstanding leverage allowed for two or more SBIC licenses under common control) to $350 million from $225 million.

---

[130] The White House, "Startup America Legislative Agenda," at http://www.whitehouse.gov/sites/default/files/uploads/startup_america_legislative_agenda.pdf.

Discussion

In 2010, the SBA announced that one of its goals for the SBIC program was to increase its "acceptance in the marketplace and increase the number of funds licensed and the amount of leverage issued so as to improve capital access for small businesses."[131] The SBA asserted that ARRA's changes to the SBIC program would help it to achieve this goal. ARRA increased the maximum leverage available to SBICs to up "to three times the private capital raised by the SBIC, or $150 million, whichever is less, and $225 million for multiple licensees under common control" and increased "the maximum leverage amounts to $175 million for single funds and $250 million for multiple funds under common control who are licensed after September 30, 2009, and invest 50% of their dollars in low income geographic areas."[132]

As mentioned previously, advocates of increasing the SBIC program's leverage limits still further and to increase the SBIC program's authorization level to $4 billion from $3 billion have argued that these actions are necessary to help fill a perceived gap in the SBA's "array of capital access programs."[133] In addition, they argue that the demise of the SBIC participating securities program and the current "underutilization" of the SBIC debentures program is preventing many small firms from accessing the capital necessary to fully realize their economic potential and assist in the national economic recovery.[134] On the other hand, others worry about the potential risk that an expanded SBIC program has for the taxpayer, especially if investments are targeted at startup and early stage small businesses which, by definition, have a more limited credit history and a higher risk for default than businesses that have established positive cash flow.

Concluding Observations

Some, including President Obama, as most recently evidenced by his Startup America Initiative, have argued that the SBA should be provided additional resources to assist small businesses in acquiring capital necessary to start, continue, or expand operations and create jobs.[135] In their view, encouraging greater utilization of the SBIC program will increase small business access to capital, result in higher levels of job creation and retention, and promote economic growth. For example, on March 19, 2012, during Senate consideration of S.Amdt. 1833, the INVEST in America Act of 2012, Senator Olympia Snowe argued

[131] U.S. Small Business Administration, "Fiscal Year 2011 Congressional Budget Justification and FY2009 Annual Performance Report," p. 52.

[132] U.S. Small Business Administration, "SBA Project Plan, Section 505: SBIC Program Changes," June 16, 2010, at http://archive.sba.gov/idc/groups/public/documents/sba_homepage/sba_sbic_plan.pdf.

[133] U.S. Congress, House Committee on Small Business, *Small Business Financing and Investment Act of 2009*, report to accompany H.R. 3854, 111th Cong., 1st sess., October 26, 2009, H.Rept. 111-315 (Washington: GPO, 2009), p. 3.

[134] U.S. Congress, House Committee on Small Business, *Full Committee Hearing on Increasing Capital for Small Business*, 111th Cong., 1st sess., October 14, 2009, House Small Business Committee Document No. 111-051 (Washington: GPO, 2009), pp. 88-91; and Representative Nydia Velázquez, "Small Business Jobs and Credit Act of 2010," House debate, *Congressional Record*, daily edition, vol. 156, no. 90 (June 16, 2010), p. H4516.

[135] Representative Nydia Velázquez, "Small Business Financing and Investment Act of 2009," House debate, *Congressional Record*, daily edition, vol. 155, no. 159 (October 29, 2009), pp. H12074, H12075; Senator Mary Landrieu, "Statements on Introduced Bills and Joint Resolutions," remarks in the Senate, *Congressional Record*, daily edition, vol. 155, no. 185 (December 10, 2009), p. S12910; The White House, "Remarks by the President on Job Creation and Economic Growth," December 8, 2009, at http://www.whitehouse.gov/the-press-office/remarks-president-job-creation-and-economic-growth; and The White House, "Startup America Legislative Agenda," at http://www.whitehouse.gov/sites/default/files/uploads/startup_america_legislative_agenda.pdf.

The amendment [S.Amdt. 1833] I and Senator Landrieu introduced would also help small companies access capital by modifying the Small Business Investment Company, SBIC, Program to raise the amount of SBIC debt the Small Business Administration, SBA, can guarantee from $3 billion to $4 billion. It would also increase the amount of SBA guaranteed debt a team of SBIC fund managers who operate multiple funds can borrow. The SBIC provisions in this amendment have bipartisan support, are noncontroversial, come at no cost to taxpayers and will create jobs. We do not get many bills of this kind in the Senate anymore.

One of the most difficult challenges facing new small businesses today is access to capital. The SBIC Program has helped companies like Apple, FedEx, Callaway Golf, and Outback Steakhouse become household names. As entrepreneurs and other aspiring small business owners well know, it takes money to make money. This legislation ensures that our entrepreneurs and high-growth companies have access to the resources they need so they can continue to drive America's economic growth and job creation in these challenging times. There is no reason why Congress should not approve this amendment to ensure capital is getting into the hands of America's job creators.

This amendment will spur investment in capital-starved startup small businesses, which will play a critical role in leading the Nation of the devastating economic down turn from which we have yet to emerge. For those who may be unfamiliar, despite significant entrepreneurial demand for small amounts of capital, because of their substantial size, most private investment funds cannot dedicate resources to transactions below $5 million. The Nation's SBICs are working to fill that gap, especially even during these challenging times.[136]

Others worry about the potential risk an expanded SBIC program may have for increasing the federal deficit. In their view, the best means to assist small business, promote economic growth, and create jobs is to reduce business taxes and exercise federal fiscal restraint.[137] For example, Representative Sam Graves, chair of the House Committee on Small Business, indicated in the Small Business Committee's FY2013 "views and estimates" letter to the House Budget Committee that the House Small Business Committee supported an increase in the SBIC program's authorization to $4 billion from $3 billion. However, he indicated that the committee opposed funding for the SBA's early stage debenture SBIC initiative and impact investment SBIC initiative because of their potential to generate losses that could lead to higher SBIC fees, or for the need to provide federal funds to subsidize the SBIC program. Representative Graves wrote in the FY2013 views and estimates letter that

The debenture SBIC program is designed to provide equity injections to small businesses that have been operational and have a track record of cash-flow and profits. ... The program is financially sound because the structure of repayments ensures that the government will not suffer significant losses. Thus, no changes are needed to the program and it operates on a zero subsidy basis without an appropriation. The SBA budget is fully supportive of this program and we concur in that recommendation, including raising the program level from $3 billion to $4 billion.

---

[136] Senator Olympia Snowe, "Jumpstart Our Business Startups Act," remarks in the Senate, *Congressional Record*, vol. 158, no. 45 (March 19, 2012), p. S15845.

[137] National Federation of Independent Business, "Payroll Tax Holiday," Washington, DC, at http://www.nfib.com/issues-elections/issues-elections-item/cmsid/49039/; and NFIB, "Government Spending," Washington, DC, at http://www.nfib.com/issues-elections/issues-elections-item/cmsid/49051/.

Presumably, some of the additional program level (which will cost the federal government no money) will be used to support two new variations in the Debenture SBIC Program [the early stage debenture SBIC initiative and the impact investment SBIC initiative] ... Neither initiative has received authority from Congress nor had its operational principles assessed by the Committee prior to implementation. The Committee reiterates its recommendation from last year's views and estimates – no funds should be allocated from the additional debenture program levels for these two programs. The Committee on the Budget also should provide further protection to the existing debenture SBIC program by requiring any modifications to the program, whether a pilot program or not, be based on a new subsidy calculation that ensures the current debenture program will operate at zero subsidy without any increase in fees due to losses stemming from the Impact and Early Stage Innovation programs.[138]

As these quotations attest, congressional debate concerning the SBIC program has primarily involved assessments of the ability of small businesses to access capital from the private sector and evaluations of the program's risk, the effect of proposed changes on the program's risk, and the potential impact of the program's risk on the federal deficit. Empirical analysis of economic data can help inform debate concerning the ability of small businesses to access capital from the private sector and the extent of the program's risk, the effect of proposed changes on the program's risk, and the potential impact of the program's risk on the federal deficit. Additional data concerning SBIC investment impact on recipient job creation and firm survival might also prove useful.

---

[138] Representative Sam Graves, "Views and Estimates of the Committee on Small Business on Matters to be set forth in the Concurrent Resolution on the Budget for Fiscal Year 2013," Washington, DC, pp. 4, 5, at http://smbiz.house.gov/ UploadedFiles/Views_and_Estimates_FY_2013.pdf. Also, see Representative Sam Graves, "Views and Estimates of the Committee on Small Business on Matters to be set forth in the Concurrent Resolution on the Budget for Fiscal Year 2012," Washington, DC, pp. 4, 5, at http://smbiz.house.gov/UploadedFiles/ March_17_Views_and_Estimates_Letter.pdf.

Appendix. Small Business Eligibility Requirements and Application Process

Small Business Eligibility Requirements

Only businesses that meet the SBA's definition of "small" may participate in the SBIC program. They must meet either the SBA's size standard for the industry in which they are primarily engaged, or a separate financial size standard that has been established for the SBIC program. SBICs use the size standard that is most likely to qualify the company, typically the financial size standard for the SBIC program. The SBIC alternative size standard is currently set as a maximum net worth of no more than $18 million and average after-tax net income for the preceding two years of not more than $6 million.[139] All of a company's subsidiaries, parent companies, and affiliates are considered in determining if it meets the size standard.

In addition, since 1997, the SBA has required SBICs to set aside a specified percentage of their financing for "businesses at the lower end of the permitted size range," primarily because "the financial size standards applicable to the SBIC program are considerably higher than those used in other SBA programs."[140] P.L. 111-5, the American Recovery and Reinvestment Act of 2009 (ARRA), requires SBICs licensed on or after the date of its enactment (February 17, 2009) to certify that at least 25% of their future financing is invested in smaller enterprises. A smaller enterprise is a company that, together with any affiliates, either has net worth of no more than $6 million and average after-tax net income for the preceding two years of no more than $2 million, or meets the SBA's size standard in the industry in which the applicant is primarily engaged.[141]

A SBIC licensed before February 17, 2009, that has not received any SBA leverage commitments after February 17, 2009, must have at least 20% of its aggregate financing dollars (plus 100% for leverage commitments over $90 million) invested in smaller enterprises.

A SBIC licensed before February 17, 2009, that has received an SBA leverage commitment after February 17, 2009, must meet the 20% threshold (plus 100% for leverage commitments over $90 million) for financing provided before the date of the first leverage commitment issued after February 17, 2009, and the 25% threshold for financing made on or after such date.[142]

SBICs are not allowed to invest in the following: other SBICs; finance and investment companies or finance-type leasing companies; unimproved real estate; companies with less than 51% of their assets and employees in the United States; passive or casual businesses (those not engaged in a regular and continuous business operation); or companies that will use the proceeds to acquire farmland.[143] In addition, SBICs may not provide funds for a small business whose primary

---

[139] 13 CFR §107.700; 13 CFR §107.710; 13 CFR §301(c)(2); and 13 CFR §301(c)(1).

[140] U.S. Small Business Administration, "Small Business Investment Companies — Leverage Eligibility and Portfolio Diversification Requirements," 74 *Federal Register* 33912, July 14, 2009.

[141] 13 CFR §107.710.

[142] U.S. Small Business Administration, "Small Business Investment Companies — Leverage Eligibility and Portfolio Diversification Requirements," 74 *Federal Register* 33912, July 14, 2009.

[143] 13 CFR §107.720.

business activity is deemed contrary to the public interest or if the funds will be used substantially for a foreign operation.[144]

Small Business Application Process

Small business owners interested in receiving SBIC financing can search for active SBICs using the SBA's SBIC directory.[145] The directory provides contact information for all licensed SBICs, sorted by state. It also includes the SBIC's preferred minimum and maximum financing size range, the type of capital provided (e.g., equity, mezzanine, subordinated debt, 1st and 2nd lien secured term, or preferred stock), funding stage preference (e.g., early stage, growing and expansion stage, or later stage), industry preference (e.g., business services, manufacturing, environmental services, or distribution), geographic preference (e.g., national, regional, or specific state or states), and a description of the firm's focus (e.g., equity capital to later stage companies for expansion and acquisition, or targeting companies with revenues of at least $5 million and profitability at the time of financing).[146]

After locating a suitable SBIC, the small business owner presents the SBIC a business plan that addresses the business's operations, management, financial condition, and funding requirements. The typical business plan includes the following information:

- the name of the business as it appears on the official records of the state or community in which it operates;

- the city, county, and state of the principal location and any branch offices or facilities;

- the form of business organization and, if a corporation, the date and state of incorporation;

- a description of the business, including the principal products sold or services rendered;

- a history of the general development of the products or services during the past five years (or since inception);

- information about the relative importance of each principal product or service to the volume of the business and to its profits;

- a description of business's real and physical property and adaptability to other business ventures;

- a description of technical attributes of its products and facilities;

- detailed information about the business's customer base, including potential customers;

- a marketing survey or economic feasibility study;

---

[144] Ibid.

[145] U.S. Small Business Administration, "All SBIC Licensees By State," at http://www.sba.gov/content/all-sbic-licensees-state.

[146] Ibid.

- a description of the distribution system for the business's products or services;

- a descriptive summary of the competitive conditions in the industry in which the business is engaged, including its competitive position relative to its largest and smallest competitors;

- a full explanation and summary of the business's pricing polices;

- brief resumes of the business's management personnel and principal owners, including their ages, education, and business experience;

- banking, business, and personal references for each member of management and for the principal owners;

- balance sheets and profit and loss statements for the last three fiscal years (or from inception);

- detailed projections of revenues, expenses, and net earnings for the coming year;

- a statement of the amount of funding requested and the time requirements for the funds;

- the reasons for the request for funds and a description of the proposed uses; and

- a description of the benefits the business expects to gain from the financing (e.g., expansion, improvement in financial position, expense reduction, or increase in efficiency).[147]

Because SBICs typically receive hundreds of business plans per year, the SBA recommends that small business owners seek a personal referral or introduction to the particular SBIC fund manager being targeted to increase "the likelihood that the business plan will be carefully considered."[148] According to the Small Business Investor Alliance, "a thorough study an SBIC must undertake before it can make a final decision could take several weeks or longer."[149]

Author Contact Information

Robert Jay Dilger
Senior Specialist in American National Government
rdilger@crs.loc.gov, 7-3110

---

[147] Small Business Investor Alliance (formerly the National Association of Small Business Investment Companies), "SBIC Financing: Step-by-Step," Washington, DC, at http://www.nasbic.org/?page=SBIC_financing.

[148] U.S. Small Business Administration, "SBIC Program," at http://www.sba.gov/content/sbic-program-0.

[149] Small Business Investor Alliance (formerly the National Association of Small Business Investment Companies), "SBIC Financing: Step-by-Step," Washington, DC, at http://www.nasbic.org/?page=SBIC_financing.

---

www.ingramcontent.com/pod-product-compliance
Lightning Source LLC
Chambersburg PA
CBHW081238170526
45165CB00009B/3104